Girls
Without
Daddies

CINDY McPIKE

Girls Without Daddies

·

Filling the Void
of a Fatherless Childhood

JORVIK
PRESS

ISBN-10: 0-9863770-6-6
ISBN-13: 978-0-9863770-6-8

Library of Congress Catalog No: 2017945109

First edition

Cover and formatting: Keith Carlson

JORVIK PRESS
5331 SW Macadam Ave., Ste 258-424
Portland OR 97239
JorvikPress.com

About the Author

After graduating from Hillsboro High School in Oregon, Cindy McPike received a BS in Business Administration from Portland State University. Her career as a certified public accountant began at one of the Big Four accounting firms. She left as a manager to become the Director of Internal Audit of a publicly traded utility. Most recently she was Chief Financial Officer of a publicly traded financial institution with over $10 billion in assets.

After taking early retirement, Ms. McPike now breeds champion Arabian and miniature horses on her ranch near Portland, Oregon. Beyond traveling and showing horses, Ms. McPike enjoys golf, particularly with her son.

For My Mother,
whose imperfect love
was perfect

Contents

1.

Who Are the Girls Without Daddies?

Why do some women seem to have it all together whereas others seem more like a butterfly trying to survive a tornado? Undoubtedly there can be countless reasons for this. In my experience, more often than not there is a common thread pulling through the fabric that weaves the behaviors of women into consistent patterns, whether directive or destructive. One of these threads can be the presence or absence of a supportive father or father figure in the adolescent lives of women. Those girls who grew up without this resource I call "girls without daddies."

Father absence can be caused by a number of factors – death, divorce, separation, abuse, neglect, emotional absence, desertion, drug or alcohol addiction, jail – or simply having never met.

Comparative statistics for children from homes with and without fathers are startling:

- Daughters who live in mother-only homes are 92% more likely to divorce.[1]

- Children age 10 to 17 living with two biological or adoptive parents were significantly less likely to experience sexual assault, child maltreatment, other types of major violence, and non-victimization type of adversity, and were less likely to witness violence in their families compared to peers living in single-parent families and stepfamilies.[2]

- Adolescents in father-absence homes were more likely to report being sexually active compared to adolescents living with their fathers.[3]

- Fatherless children are at a dramatically greater risk of drug and alcohol abuse.[4]

- Between 18% and 25% of children have no contact with their fathers two to three years after a divorce.[5]

Further, children from fatherless homes are 15.3 times more likely to have behavioral disorders:

- 4.6 times more likely to commit suicide

- 6.6 times more likely to become teenage mothers

- 24.3 times more likely to run away

- 6.3 times more likely to be in state-operated institutions

- 6.6 times more likely to drop out of school.

- 15.3 times more likely to end up in prison as a teenager.[6]

Sadly, the number of girls who fall into the category of fatherless homes is on the rise. According to the US Census Bureau, out of about 12 million single-parent families in 2015, more than 80% were headed by single mothers.[7]

The delineated harshness of these statistics is difficult for most to believe. So how much easier is it for a girl without a daddy to rationalize away this reality?

For many years I blinded myself to the consequences of being without a supportive father figure. Only in hindsight was it obvious how these statistics might apply to me. Although I had a father and a stepfather, my father was not present and my stepfather's influence was destructive. Throughout my youth and young adult years, I exhibited behaviors that didn't feel quite balanced. That I might not be whole was difficult to consider, as the last thing I wanted was to think myself ill-equipped to deal with life. I wanted to be a normal, well-balanced individual.

Regardless, I knew deep down that something was missing. Ultimately, after this introspection, I concluded I am indeed a girl without a daddy despite the alleged presence of two father figures, because neither was a healthy influence on me in my adolescent years.

If you are a girl without a daddy or a single mother, don't let the statistics cause you despair. You (and your children) certainly are not doomed. Recognizing the linkage between certain behavioral patterns and their underlying cause is a substantial contributor toward moving past potentially destructive behaviors to a healthy self-esteem, healthy relationships and healthy life decisions.

Each chapter of this book is designed to identify common behavioral patterns in women that grew up without healthy father figures in their lives. Not all patterns will manifest for every woman and certainly those that do might manifest in varied forms of those presented here.

You might like to keep notes about which patterns are or are not relevant to you, or perhaps relevant to a loved one for whom you are reading this book, and how the relevant patterns might differ in your personal situation. After finishing the book, you might review your notes and use them to identify personal crutches you might have developed. Then, assess whether these crutches might be negatively affecting your relationships and decisions and are actually more damaging than helpful.

For me, identifying the behavior was often a substantial part of the battle, but there were times when pushing past old behaviors was scary and took a couple tries before a new habit was developed. Everyone reacts differently, but understanding what makes us tick is a great first step toward personal growth.

My hope is that this book helps you along your path toward personal growth more quickly than the time it took me to fill the holes my absent father left, and that in this book you find at least one "golden nugget" that contributes substantially to your personal growth and lifelong happiness.

2.

Breaking Up is Hard to Do

I've not met many people that look forward to the discussion that follows the words: "We need to talk." Breaking up is difficult even for emotionally healthy people, as it should be. It shouldn't be easy to end a relationship if it involves breaking someone's heart. But is it more difficult for girls without daddies to break up with their romantic partners than it is for girls with daddies – and if so, why?

As a teenager and young woman, breaking up was not my forte. If I managed to break up, I'd inevitably seek out or be amenable to a reconciliation. This pattern of behavior was not obvious to me until it occurred in a relationship that was clearly more trouble than it was worth. I doubted I loved the guy. In fact I wasn't sure I liked him. Yet every time we broke up I'd later agree to get back together with him. The disparity between my feelings and my actions compelled me to acknowledge that something was in charge that had nothing to do with the relationship.

I decided to seek professional counseling to determine why I couldn't leave a problematic relationship. At the time this move was scary because I felt like I was admitting inadequacy. Now I consider it a bold step and one of the best decisions I ever made. In the counselling sessions I began describing my dilemma and the gory details of my relationship.

Of course, that description included a multitude of stories with detailed specifics about all the different ways I had been wronged by this guy. But, my summary description of the problem to the counselor was that I couldn't understand the angst the breakup(s) caused, since my feelings for the guy were mixed at best. Why couldn't I make a clean break?

My counselor's response to this question was to inquire about my childhood. I told her what little came to mind and she asked me to give it some more thought for our next session. Before our next meeting I spent some time talking to a few family members to gather more information. The only revelation was that my lack of memories about my mother were largely because she worked so much. In hindsight, I could see that was true. She was unhappy in her marriage to my stepfather and work was her escape.

I didn't require input regarding memories of my abusive stepfather or my absent father. The former memories were sadly something I was unable to forget. My absent biological father, a guy that lived fifteen minutes away, offered few memories simply because I only saw him a couple of times a year. I never thought much about my biological father's absence but my sister was tormented by his lack of interest in us. I simply knew him for what he was – a man who just didn't have an interest in children, not even his own. I didn't personalize it. I didn't feel any pain from it. It had nothing to do with me. He was just not a great draw for a father. That is what I believed.

At my next appointment I added the new information about my childhood. As I spoke, I watched the look on my counselor's face, which made it clear that I had confirmed some theory she had formed.

She looked at me and said, "You were abandoned as a child."

I was a little startled by her odd conclusion. I had lived with my mom. I saw my dad a couple of times a year and his absence had nothing to do with me. How was I abandoned? Yet, the independent perspective of a professional counselor made me ponder the deeper influence my home life may have had on me. It seemed my perspective while growing up may have eliminated my recognition of the negative impact that my draw of a daddy had on me.

But that perspective did not fill the void created by the absence of a loving father figure in my adolescent life.

I began to understand the differences I observed in my behavior compared to those lucky girls who grew up with loving fathers. With this new-found perspective, I began my path toward wholeness.

This path started with addressing what the counselor called a pit of sadness in my presence. I asked her how to get rid of it. She just smiled and said that I'd have to cry a lot. I didn't like that answer and asked for another way. She smiled and said there was no other way.

I left the session concerned that the counselor might be right. I had ignored this void, but it had not ignored me. I was assigned the worst homework imaginable. I could no longer excuse my father for just being who he was. I had to face the reality that his absence actually hurt me.

I did not set out to judge my father, who had died years earlier. Instead, I looked through my history with the unbiased perspective the counselor provided, thinking through as much life experience as I could, watching memories as if they were an inner video of someone else's life. I adjusted my perspective away from how I had viewed my father's absence and instead viewed my origins from the alternate perspective my counselor offered – that I had been abandoned. This was my move into a new paradigm.

Among the memories was one in particular. At a time when my stepfather was making things particularly tough at home, my mother told me to go over to talk to my dad. I remember being excited because there was some hope my dad might help. I didn't know what my father was going to say or do, but he must care enough that I was having troubles because I was going over to talk to him about them.

I got to his house. We sat at the kitchen table. My father told me that my mom had called to tell him that things at home with her were difficult. Then he said those words a little girl never wants to hear from her father. He said I couldn't live with him because his wife would never allow it but if I wanted to move out of my mom's house and live on my own he would give me the $50 a month in child support that he currently paid her. I was 16 years old. It was laughable. I can't even remember how I responded. In fact, I don't remember speaking at all – but I do remember a deep sense of emptiness and hopelessness. Talk about abandonment.

The complete exercise of reviewing my memories took weeks, even longer, as occasionally memories would pop in my head and I'd proceed to give them their due. I processed a few memories at a time, took a breather and then resumed. Many of the reviewed items were of absentee moments, otherwise the process would have been brief, given that my biological father had little interaction with me.

Many past circumstances and issues that sprang to mind I had handled on my own, when many teenage girls would have Velcro parents forcing help down their daughters' throats. At a time when I was least equipped to make decisions, the decisions I faced had potential for lifelong consequences – parties, alcohol, drugs and sex, just to name a few.

How different so many things would have been if I had a loving father there talking to me, guiding me, making me feel valued and important. I thought of times my girlfriends talked of things their fathers had done for them and faced the ache I ignored so many years ago. To those who suffered the same void as me, this will make tremendous sense. The reality set in. What the counselor called abandonment I thought of as the void left where a positive male influence should have been in my life.

After these trips down memory lane and more conversations with the counselor, I understood why it was so hard to walk away from relationships, even unhealthy ones. I needed to hang on to my relationships with men because I didn't want to feel abandoned again.

Failing in a relationship with a man brought a familiar hopelessness and insecurity. What I was getting from those unhealthy relationships had nothing to do with the man involved at all. It was simply that he was a man. I was selling my chances for a healthy relationship by settling for the man I was with regardless of my actual interest in the man or how unhealthy the relationship might be.

This phenomenon was not unique to me. Women who have been abandoned by their fathers tend to cling to their significant others, because they fear being abandoned once again.[1]

What was the difference between me and a girl with a daddy? They are more likely to have a secure attachment style, where I had an insecure attachment style. When a child forms a secure attachment, she is able to have meaningful relationships as an adult, to be empathetic and set appropriate boundaries. A secure attachment occurs when the parental style is aligned with the child and in tune with the child's emotions.[2]

What causes the attachment style to be insecure? Insecure attachment can result when the parent is unavailable, inconsistent, or when the child is ignored, or when the parent is too attached or otherwise not functioning properly.[3]

Adults with insecure attachment can be self-critical and insecure, seek approval from others (although the reinforcement is unlikely to be effective), fear rejection (and even look for signs of rejection), have difficulty trusting, act clingy and be overly dependent on their partner.[4]

Is insecure attachment a life sentence to dysfunctional romantic relationships? It wasn't for me. Case studies suggest the same is true for others. If you are able to process negative childhood experiences you can prevent them from inhibiting your ability to form healthy relationships as an adult.[5]

My newfound knowledge, combined with the fruits of reviewing memories, allowed me to begin effectively assessing relationships. I learned that I had to find my self-confidence independently of relationships with men. I was an adult and the opportunities to learn those things from my father were forever gone, if they ever existed.

At that point in my life I had developed a few strong friendships that I could lean on while building up self-esteem. I couldn't exactly make myself immediately whole, but in short order I was able to remedy my outlook enough to keep a better perspective on whether the current relationship was worth the effort.

When the negatives outweighed the positives, rather than hanging on out of fear of failure or rejection I could now walk away confidently. Of course, breakups are always painful. There is inevitably some good in each relationship whose loss is mourned. By refusing to impose the fear of failure and sense of rejection on top of that pain, I was able to make healthy decisions about the relationship. When it was time to get out, I could make a clean break and not look back, because I had enough confidence to realize it was the best decision for both of us.

This also served as a greater kindness to men I dated. Rather than stringing someone along, I could break off the relationship early rather than letting the guy develop emotions, even though I was only in the relationship because I just couldn't walk away.

To prevent yourself from being doomed to a pattern of clinging to failed relationships, embark on a journey of processing negative childhood experiences. After my journey, the first time I made a clean break I felt like I had achieved something monumental.

This might sound trivial to those who grew up with supportive father figures, but I'm proud to say I earned that monument despite the absence of my daddy.

You deserve a fantastically healthy romantic relationship but you might need to work on yourself before you can achieve this goal. The goal should be a relationship where one plus one adds up to more than two. That equation leaves you and your romantic partner energy to give back to the world rather than the relationship sucking the life out of you both.

3.

Will You Always Feel Fatherless?

You may take on grown up responsibilities – marriage, children, job – living day by day and dealing with the responsibilities you assumed. Yet emotional vulnerability occasionally produces a childlike feeling. Why? There are key differences between feeling grown up and being emotionally mature. We'll explore those differences and seek paths to personal development, paying special attention to the additional challenges girls without daddies might have to face.

Feeling grown up typically occurs when people reach key milestones, such as buying a home, marriage and/or having a child.[1] Thus feeling grown up is a result of a person's actions and various external factors. For example, whether or not a person lands a job is a function of both. While we can control our actions, we cannot control all the external factors that also play a role.

So what happens when the conditions that made someone feel grown up are reversed? For example, they lose their job or lose their house. While feeling grown up might provide some sense of accomplishment or give an impression of maturity, it's too shallow to be a meaningful, consistent source of emotional stability.

Emotional maturity originates from within and therefore its inherent nature is not as easily ruffled by the inevitable roadblocks and challenges we all encounter in life. What is emotional maturity? Wikipedia defines maturity as "the ability to respond to the environment in an appropriate manner. This response is generally learned rather than instinctive." Emotional maturity is further defined as "a higher state of self-awareness."[2] How does one achieve this?

The journey progresses through several levels:

- Level 1. Basic emotional responsibility: you quit blaming external factors and stop being a victim.

- Level 2. Emotional honesty: you begin to own your feelings. Self-discovery begins.

- Level 3. Emotional openness: you begin to share your feelings. Self-disclosure begins.

- Level 4. Emotional assertiveness: you begin to ask for and receive emotional nurturing.

- Level 5. Emotional understanding: you begin to understand the cause and effect of emotional responsibility. Self-knowledge begins.

- Level 6. Emotional detachment: you are freed from self-concepts imposed by others. Unconditional love is possible.[3]

Once you achieve level 6, you're no longer a butterfly in a tornado. Your stability comes from within because you accept your own imperfections – and you accept the imperfections of others. You're able to grow and learn emotionally because you can discuss feelings openly and ask for help when you need it. You are no longer at the whim of others' opinions about how you should be or what you should do.

Does the presence or absence of a supportive father figure influence the development of emotional maturity? Studies show that it does. Father involvement is positively correlated with children's overall social competence, social initiative, social maturity, and capacity for relatedness with others.[4] Further, children of involved fathers are more likely to have positive peer relations.[5]

These attributes would not be possible without emotional maturity. Father absence will likely challenge and possibly impede the achievement of this level of personal development.

Many years ago, a friend of mine opened my eyes to the illusive feelings of emotional maturity by pointing out how differently she would feel if she were in my shoes. In my early thirties I had a baby in my arms and found myself headed toward divorce. I was at work, crying to this girlfriend, scared about everything, feeling unloved, blah, blah, blah. Then I realized my girlfriend was smiling. Irritated with her amused attitude about my hardship, I expressed my unhappiness.

She continued smiling and simply said, "It's nice to be forty." She went on to say that things like this just didn't matter as much when you are forty years old. I asked if she seriously expected me to believe that if I were her age and my marriage was falling apart and I had a tiny baby in my arms, I wouldn't be as devastated. She smiled and assured me I wouldn't be.

Her confidence led me to look forward to my fortieth birthday like never before! As it turns out, she was right. I can look back at the tumultuous period that divorce represented and honestly say that if it happened today I'd be absolutely fine. In fact, I'd likely have booted a partner out the door before he had a chance to leave on his own accord.

So have I achieved emotional maturity? Whenever I say that I've evolved to that level, my son always adds that I'm humble as well! But for the most part I'm able to deflect the nonsense that people might throw my way, whether intentional or not. For example, when I was younger if someone was rude to me I'd take it personally. Now, after a quick moment of thought, I conclude the person is either terribly unhappy or having a bad day.

As you make your way through life you encounter real problems, like friends getting cancer and facing major surgeries, radiation and chemotherapy. If faced with the choice of watching a friend deal with those things or hearing my spouse say he didn't love me anymore, I'd choose the latter in a heartbeat. Being emotionally mature allows you to evaluate alleged issues to determine whether they are worthy of your energy.

In short, feeling grown up is like being on a teeter-totter. How high and low you go is only partly within your control. However, emotional maturity brings an internal sense of wholeness and peace not subject to external manipulation. With it, your response to efforts by others to manipulate you will be a simple smile and perhaps a tad bit of empathy for the shortcomings reflected in their attempts at manipulation.

Instead of feeling like a little girl, you can instead be a little girl at heart and enjoy the simple pleasures in life because you are able to ignore the noise around you. The next few chapters attempt to lay out a pathway to achieving growth toward emotional maturity.

4.

Judgement Causes Pain

The weak can never forgive.
Forgiveness is the attribute of the strong.

Mahatma Gandhi

As noted, the first level of emotional maturity is basic emotional responsibility, an inner state that girls without daddies have more difficulty in attaining. Deficits in this level often manifest as coping mechanisms, such as blaming others, and a pattern of subjecting oneself to victimization.

How does a fatherless woman overcome her disadvantage? The first step is determining whether she has adopted coping mechanisms that sadly result in unhealthy behavioral patterns. The second step is eliminating the need for these coping mechanisms by accepting responsibility for her emotions. Here we'll focus on the first step to emotional responsibility. This involves ceasing to blame others by understanding how this reaction can actually create the pain that its purpose was to avoid.

In my counseling sessions I would drone on about all the awful things that had been done to me and how much pain had resulted. In short, I was blaming other people for my unhappiness. The counselor patiently listened. After she'd heard enough, she said something to me that I've repeated many times to people who have shared their pain with me. She said that sometimes the pain in life doesn't come from what people do to us but comes from our judgement of what they do to us. I left that session and decided to test this concept.

I reviewed some of the most painful things people had "done to me." Instead of judging what people had done by assuming their goal was to hurt me, I asked myself what might be going on with the person that caused them to behave carelessly.

The counselor was right. There was less pain. Don't get me wrong. I believe there are evil people in this world, but for the most part I now believe that many of the people we allow in our lives that inevitably hurt us never set out to do so. They might be ignorant, and resultantly do something hurtful. They might be in pain themselves and as a result say or do something hurtful. They might be dealing with some need and fill it up at someone else's expense.

Most often I believe people are so preoccupied with their own needs that they are completely unaware of how their actions impact others. Essentially, those we consider perpetrators might feel under attack for reasons we do not comprehend. As a result, they throw out survival bombs and we're just in the way of where those bombs land.

What the counselor's statement did was begin my process of ceasing to blame external factors for my unhappiness by giving me another way of looking at its origin. My example on this point involves a dear friend, who at the time had been my friend for over fifteen years. We are still friends and will be until one of us dies.

She had been my boss and had just been promoted into a position in a field new to her. I was moved up into her previous position. She kept bragging to my new boss (her old boss) that she was continuing to help me. These statements really bothered me because I felt the implication was that I was not yet competent to do my new job. In hindsight perhaps she was right, but at the time I was still cocky, something I fortunately matured past as I realized how much more there is to know about life.

I was working late one night, sitting in my office looking out the window at the city lights, pondering this situation. I just couldn't figure out why she would "do this to me." She had been such a perfect friend for so many years. In fact, she was the person in my life that taught me what friendship really meant. I would have been lost without her friendship.

How could she jeopardize my career by bragging at my expense? If I previously hadn't been in counseling and hadn't had this concept of judgement causing pain planted in my head, I wonder whether I would have been able to step outside the hurt enough to see through the situation.

Fortunately, as a result of my counseling I recognized that I might be creating my own pain by judging her actions. Between that realization and knowing that my friend truly loved me and would never intentionally hurt me, I forced myself past my hurt to consider my friend's needs and how they might be driving her actions. It was simple. Her actions weren't about me at all. She felt insecure in her new position and felt the need to make sure people knew that while she was getting up to speed in her new role she was still adding value by helping me.

I was so hurt by her actions because I judged them. When I realized her needs were so great she couldn't even see that she might be hurting me, it simply didn't hurt anymore. In fact, my thoughts went more toward what she was going through. I sucked up my pride and let her have what she needed. Time would show I could do my job, and time would show she could do her new job just fine, too. The situation would self-correct so I decided to do nothing about it. I never told her because telling her would have hurt her at an obviously vulnerable time. She had done so much for me over the years it seemed the least I could give back was to support her in this way. As expected, with a little time everything worked out fine for both of our careers.

After applying the words of wisdom from my counselor to this situation, I started to review other painful experiences in my life where I was the alleged victim. I suppose it was a residual effort on my part to get rid of my pit of sadness, as described by my counselor. Reviewing the mental videos of the wrongs done to me, I could see that many of the alleged wrongs were really situations where I was more of an innocent bystander than the target of a wrongdoer's evil.

Here's another example of misinterpreting someone's intent. Early in my career, I had just separated from my first husband. It was a young marriage and a relationship that I should have walked away from before the marriage (those old abandonment issues). A woman I worked with had discovered my separated status and asked me how long I had been married. I told her it was two years. She then bluntly said, "That wasn't very long." Wasn't very long? Easy for her to say, as it seemed like an eternity of hell to me. To her blunt comment I simply replied, "F*** you!" I admit it wasn't my finest moment. When I saw the look on her face after my retort I felt awful.

She was completely clueless as to how offensive her comment was. She went on to apologize profusely. It was only because I was in my work mode of thought that I could defend myself. If it had been anywhere else I would have shrunk up inside and felt hurt that she could say something so cruel. While her comment wasn't very thoughtful, her intent was not to be cruel. She just didn't think it through and had no personal experience to comprehend how offensive her statement was.

As the years rolled by, I learned this was a common problem for her, which not surprisingly resulted in occasional career challenges. What seemed a harsh and cruel comment directed to hurt me was really just ignorance spewing out of someone's mouth.

I believe it would be remiss to write all this about how judgement can cause pain and not take a moment to reflect on the fact that there are real jerks in the world. True jerks are narcissists.

This is how the Mayo Clinic website defines this condition: "If you have narcissistic personality disorder, you may come across as conceited, boastful or pretentious. You often monopolize conversations. You may belittle or look down on people you perceive as inferior. You may feel a sense of entitlement – and when you don't receive special treatment, you may become impatient or angry… At the same time, you have trouble handling anything that may be perceived as criticism. You may have secret feelings of insecurity, shame, vulnerability and humiliation. To feel better, you may react with rage or contempt and try to belittle the other person to make yourself appear superior. Or you may feel depressed and moody because you fall short of perfection."[1]

My oversimplification of this is that jerks act out irrationally due to underlying insecurities, whether they realize it or not. This is not an excuse for their behavior, but rather an explanation. Knowing what causes their behavior might lessen the pain a bit, but it's likely going to be a fixed pattern of behavior. Therefore, when a person you're dealing with is truly a jerk you have two choices: be a victim or get away from them.

The personalization of others' behavior patterns puts our happiness in the hands of people that may or may not have intended to cause us pain. Recognizing that many misunderstandings begin in the mist between one person's mouth and another person's ear aids our ability to step outside of what appears to be a painful situation and analyze it.

When a girl without a daddy changes her first thought from assuming negative intent by others to wondering what might be going on in the other person's life, she begins a journey which ends with knowing her happiness cannot be destroyed by the words or actions of others. This thought process is a tool that aids her in ceasing to blame others and enables her to take responsibility for her emotions. Food for thought – how many people have you hurt without realizing it?

5.

Are You a Victim?

The second part of achieving emotional responsibility is learning to stop being a victim. In this chapter we are not addressing emotional, physical or sexual abuse, but rather self-victimization.

Self-victimization's origins come from learned helplessness that begins in childhood. Children are at the mercy of others. If that so-called mercy includes suboptimal parenting, neglect, abuse or other negative factors, then the child has no choice but to make the best of a bad situation.

That's fine for a child. The problems arise when this behavior continues into adulthood.[1] When girls without daddies continue this coping mechanism as adults, they "allow" themselves to continue to be victimized. Eliminating this negative behavioral pattern involves first identifying it and then replacing it with healthy behaviors.

My mother has what I call a servant's heart. I view this as a spiritual gift. She'll do anything for anybody. I, on the other hand, was not blessed with that gift. It is not in my nature to serve. Even so, somehow I still ended up giving, even when I really didn't want to give, particularly in romantic relationships. It didn't matter whether the request was big or small. I'd try to say what I wanted but if it met with resistance I'd buckle in a heartbeat.

There must be ten thousand examples of this but they all seem so petty now, so here are just two. Petty example number one: during my college years if I had a big test coming up but my boyfriend had "important" plans for us, I resisted, folded and then complained to others. Petty example number two – if I wanted to take an evening to myself but the guy I was dating insisted we do something together, I resisted, folded and then complained to others. And so on. Each time I folded, the wall between me and the other person in the relationship would grow until the damage was potentially irreparable.

What is the difference between someone with a servant's heart and a victim? In my opinion, a person with a servant's heart has a true spiritual gift. If everyone had this gift, I suppose we'd achieve what has never been achieved, a theoretically pure state of communism. People would be falling all over themselves to give. True giving holds no account of the past. When a person with a servant's heart gives, they smile at the good they have done and move on.

However, a victim is one who subjugates her desires to the desires of others out of insecurity, the need for acceptance, or simply because they don't know how to do otherwise (learned helplessness). When a person "gives" for these reasons, her friends are likely to hear phrases like, "They always do this to me," "They never think about me," "Can you believe they even asked me to do that?" An even worse case scenario is the sad-hearted person who simply gives up and is too hopeless to even complain about it. These women are unknowingly self-created victims, servants without seemingly having a choice, slaves to whatever people ask of them.

In my opinion, self-victimization is the most common behavioral pattern observable in girls without daddies. Throughout childhood, they've been taught that their desires, opinions or wants don't matter. A person with this background doesn't believe she can have any control in these matters, which is why she keeps getting sucked into relationships with users that take advantage of her. Her giving isn't a choice. It's a default pattern continued from childhood.

She becomes the victim that keeps a negative balance in her account and can only cry in her heart. I am not criticizing victims here but rather attempting to help them see their possible culpability in their own victimization. The goal is to find the resources to assert control and limit this negative behavioral pattern.

In the childhood home environment of a girl with a daddy, the supportive father figure establishes ways for girls to learn their self-worth and communicate their needs. In those homes healthy patterns of give and take are demonstrated regularly. There is open communication and appropriate balancing of wants and needs.

The father further teaches the daughter to assert herself through experiences with people outside the family. A teenage girl is going on a date and the boy honks his horn from the curb. The girl's loving father figure persuades her to wait in the house until the boy realizes she does not answer to a horn. That girl's father just taught her she is worth something.

A teenage girl has a part-time job after school and her boss (a teenage boy) is harassing her. The girl with a supportive father figure is shown how to deal with the boy, which teaches her that she needs to stand up for herself. "Having a father present is how she develops immeasurable skills that will help her become assertive, proactive, productive and creative as she grows into adulthood."[2]

In the childhood home of a girl without a daddy, there may be suboptimal circumstances which result in no venting of needs or wants, let alone appropriate balancing of them. There may be no sense that the little girl counts at all. If a boy honks from his car, she may not want to risk his rejecting her when she stands up for what any self-respecting girl should expect. Instead, she runs out to the car so the boy doesn't have to wait too long for her.

In the case of an abusive boss, she'll apologize for whatever the perceived offense might be. If it's a case of sexual harassment, she'll certainly be inclined to give in and go on a date. This self-silencing of needs can build toward a pattern of victimization if continued into adulthood. Obviously, not all women should be taught to be fist-pounding egomaniacs that always get what they believe they are due. The point is that when a person doesn't feel comfortable expressing her wants or desires, then giving is a default pattern, not a choice.

My personal experience of giving by default is a case in point. I certainly was not as happy as I could have been in early relationships. Conceivably, the guys were not at fault. Usually, they didn't know I was giving something that I didn't want to give, because I didn't have the self-confidence to address it. I'd instead complain about it to my female friends, whose judgement I did not fear. If my relationship had a chance, my self-silencing doomed it. I temporarily protected the little girl inside me, but from every other perspective my giving did more harm than good.

Some people believe that asserting one's needs is selfish and self-serving. I've even been cautioned against the evils of professional counselors because they teach you to give your needs consideration, presumably to the exclusion of the needs of others. If a person dooms a relationship through self-silencing, is that loving? Sometimes the more loving act is to make your needs known.

I had to find the path that would enable me to limit my overgiving. First, let me relate an extreme example of standing up for myself.

It was the fortunate end of an emotionally abusive relationship that started in my youth, my first marriage. By emotionally abusive I mean comments like, "What is wrong with you," "You are a pig," or physically slamming things around or breaking them without actually hitting me.

At one point, my "romantic" partner raised his hand to hit me. I put my chin out and said, "Do it! I'd love to have a physical bruise to show people." In the middle of one of these verbal assaults I could suddenly hear myself think, "I wouldn't let a stranger say that to me."

Those walls around me tumbled down and I stepped out of my little-girl veil and said: "Enough!" It was an epiphany. If I was going to survive, I had to stand up for myself. In the midst of the verbal berating I held my hand up like a stop sign and said, "I'm done."

Even given my later accomplishments, I believe this was one of the most powerful moments of my life. I stood up to the beast.

Where did that sense of self-worth come from? In my case, from a surrogate father figure. My first job at sixteen was in a large retail store. The store manager was a kind man of fatherly age. In my mind, he was this super-powerful, well balanced, all-knowing man. For whatever reason, he took me under his wing.

One day in customer service an irate female customer was giving me a verbal tongue lashing. I figured customers always know best so I stood there and took it. My father figure hero walked up, interrupted the woman's rant and took control of the situation. He didn't listen to anything the angry customer had to say, telling her abruptly to take her business elsewhere.

Then in that key moment in my life, he turned, looked directly in my face and said firmly, "Don't ever let anyone talk to you like that again."

Immediately after saying that he walked away. I was a bit surprised because it was almost like he was mad at me because I hadn't stood up for myself.

His was the voice I heard on that day I broke free from an abusive relationship. I saw myself through my surrogate father figure's eyes and suddenly just knew I deserved better. It might sound simple, but a "father" rushing to my defense showed me how to begin building the edifice of my self-worth.

Even so, I continued to be a victim in less extreme situations. But now I had finally identified my own contribution to my unhappiness – over-giving – so I could set out a path to remedying that behavior.

Step one was to own my part in the problem by taking responsibility for my emotions and acknowledging how much damage my over-giving had caused. A typical example of this reaction was getting upset with people when all they did was ask and all I did was say yes. I had damaged relationships by not asking for what I wanted and by failing to say no to the things I didn't want. Then I would punish friends by making them listen to me whine about how someone treated me. Self-silencing and the resultant over-giving were hurting me and those around me.

Step two was to understand why I hadn't mustered the power to stop myself from over-giving. In short, I didn't believe my needs were worthy and I was afraid that standing up for what I wanted would result in my losing a relationship. I was basically continuing to act like a little girl without the power to change things.

Simply acknowledging those two factors was huge. I followed up by replacing these childlike thoughts with positive self-talk, telling myself repeatedly that what I wanted mattered and hiding my true feelings would only cause more problems in the long run.

But I also had to accept that asserting myself put me at greater risk of rejection.

Step three was to put one foot in front of the other and proceed. It took much practice, trial and error, and more than a few moments of weakness that by default turned into failure before I found the right balance.

Here are some of those little steps:

- When I felt that sinking pit in my stomach, I'd stop and pay attention to it. What was it saying? It was telling me I was unhappy with whatever was happening.

- I'd bravely trust the other person enough to tell them how I was feeling. If this met with resistance, I'd try to stand my ground. If resistance continued I'd say I needed some time to think about it so I could diffuse the situation and take time to build up the courage to try again.

- I'd try again. If I had to try too many times, then perhaps self-silencing wasn't the problem. Perhaps the relationship's viability needed to be reevaluated.

When you are making these changes, remember to be fair to the people in your life and let them know what you're trying to accomplish. Explain that, potentially through no fault of theirs, you've not been as open as you need to be for the health of the relationship and that you are beginning a process of changing that by expressing your wants and needs more than you might have in the past. Whether or not you owe this courtesy is irrelevant because a sudden shift in your behavior is likely to bring resistance, and potentially aggression, at a time when you're just beginning to learn to stand up for yourself. If you can eliminate some of that resistance in advance, your progress will be less bumpy and more successful.

What did I learn on my journey to end my days of victimhood? I learned the true joy of giving. When I said yes, I gave with my whole heart and did not hold a record of what I had done. In fact, I didn't even care if the person might have been taking advantage of me. My giving resulted in a smile and a heart full of joy.

As a child, a girl without a daddy might not have learned that her wants or needs count. As a result she might have adopted a behavior of learned helplessness and self-silencing that has led to self-victimization. Recognizing this negative behavior pattern and accepting responsibility for it will end her days of self-victimization and lead to emotional responsibility.

6.

Own Your Feelings

The next level of emotional maturity is emotional honesty. In order to be honest with yourself about your feelings, you must first believe your feelings are valid and then you must own them. We will look at why girls without daddies might have more impediments to achieving these two steps compared to those lucky girls with supportive father figures. Then we will address how girls without daddies can overcome these impediments and reach the goal of emotional honesty.

Belief in the validity of one's emotions is learned in childhood. Legitimizing a child's feelings is imperative because it builds her self-esteem and reduces defiant behavior.[1] Defiant behavior might be an understatement. One quick way to get the hair to stand up on the back of my neck is to tell me that I shouldn't be upset about what I'm upset about.

Not coincidentally, legitimizing feelings is a tactic that well-trained customer service representatives often employ. They will listen to the problem without interrupting. When the upset customer has expressed their dissatisfaction and/or anger, the agent will say, "I'm so sorry that happened to you," or something that makes the customer feel understood and legitimized. (Verizon is great at this!) This takes the customer off the defensive, enabling them participate in developing or agreeing to a resolution. When these feelings are not legitimized, the customer remains stuck at the beginning of the process because they first want to be understood.

If the world was full of great customer service agents then none of us would need to own our feelings, because we could rely on everyone else to do it for us. Alas, the world just isn't made that way. We must help ourselves.

Unfortunately, children who were not taught by their parents that their feelings are valid may not have the level of self-esteem necessary to legitimize their own feelings. Girls without daddies are more likely to have this disadvantage because their childhood circumstances bring a greater risk of suboptimal parenting.

The key is to learn that your feelings, no matter what they are, are valid simply because they are your feelings. If your childhood or current environment lack validation, then learn to validate yourself. This begins with self-praise. Whenever you do something positive, praise yourself. If you've committed to working out regularly and you do so, praise yourself. Begin a habit of self-validation. This habit will aid you in accepting your feelings, whatever they might be.

What is the benefit of validating our feelings? I used to have this pet peeve over line cutting. It used to make my blood boil if someone stepped into line in front of me. Are those feelings valid? They certainly are. If I attempt to deny those feelings and bury them deep inside, I'm likely headed to high blood pressure or an early heart attack. Alternatively, I can acknowledge my feelings and accept them as valid.

Of course, not all feelings should be acted upon. Just because my feelings are valid doesn't give me permission to grab the offender and slam them to the ground. What good does it do me, then, to validate my irritation in this situation? Knowing my feelings are valid allows me to cease boiling my own blood and simply say to the offender, "Excuse me, but I was here first." Now, that's a lot of progress compared to wanting to grab someone and throw them to the ground! Through that sense of power I felt over the situation, I also learned to occasionally take a step back and let the person cut in.

The second step in owning your feelings is to recognize that no one can make you feel anything. Consider:

"External events and people cannot make us feel any one certain way, even though it often seems that way. We enter into every situation with certain beliefs or expectations. Those beliefs and expectations directly influence the way we are going to end up feeling about the event or person... In other words, our beliefs and expectations about a person or event or situation directly influence and, many would argue, cause our feelings. They are not the result of or inherent in the situation itself. Others do not cause our feelings – we cause them ourselves."[2]

The concept of owning one's feelings was first taught to me in the workplace many years ago. Our employee group was called into a conference room for mandatory team-building training. In one exercise the trainer would make statements and then solicit our responses.

One statement was, "You made me mad." Then we were to describe our reactions to that statement. The point was twofold. First, it was a terrible way to start an open-ended conversation. More importantly, no one can make you feel anything. We feel and react based on our own experiences and therefore we must own our feelings.

Initially, I absolutely did not agree with her. But since the mandatory training went on without any concern for my opinion, I was forced to think about the trainer's message through the subsequent exercises she set forth.

In the end I agreed. No one can make me feel anything. They may say things and as a result I have a reaction or feeling based on my prior experiences and my interpretation of what I heard.

In this workplace exercise we were taught to change how we verbalized our feelings. Instead of saying, "You made me angry," we were to say, "When you said that, I felt angry." The exercise had two purposes. One, we needed to own our unique emotional reactions to statements made by others because we might have misinterpreted the meaning based on our prior experiences. Second, by owning our emotional reaction we do not place the blame on the other person and are therefore less likely to end up with them being defensive. In other words, owning our feelings is essential to working through conflict (conflict management is addressed in the next chapter).

I'll give you a simple example of owning my feelings. My son had a friend coming to the house and together they were going to a basketball game. He asked me to stay upstairs when his friend arrived. Of course, my initial reaction was to be offended!

Did I say, "That really hurts my feelings. Am I really that embarrassing that you don't want me to meet your friends?"

No. I simply owned my reaction and asked, "Why do you want me to stay upstairs?"

His answer? His friend was a girl but not a girlfriend and he would feel more comfortable if I didn't make a big deal out of his friend being a girl. Simple enough. I doubt I would have made a big deal out of it. Regardless, by not making his statements and actions about me, but rather by owning my feelings before I asked his reasoning, we were able to skip a lot of drama and get to a good understanding of what, if any, thinking was behind his request.

When you own your reactions, your disclosure of your feelings ceases to be accusatory. Non-confrontational communication leads more quickly to a clearer understanding of what is happening. In my transitional period to owning my feelings, I couldn't immediately skip putting a little blame in my approach and I'd say something like, "I kind of let my feelings get hurt when you asked me to go upstairs before your friend arrived, but then I wondered if maybe your asking really didn't have anything to do with me. Is that the case?"

When I took that approach, I'd often see the look of surprise on the other person's face and I could tell they either simply didn't think about how they worded their statement or that their wording was driven by their own defensiveness. Seeing surprised faces a few times helped me skip this step as I realized how frequently the "offender" meant no offense ("Judgement Causes Pain"). They were like me, a fallible human being who doesn't always express herself perfectly, often letting my own defensiveness drive my delivery.

And so, accepting your own human fallibility also helps you accept it in others, and thus helps your overall relationships. Knowing that you are not perfect keeps your mind open to the fact that other people make mistakes too. Don't get me wrong, there are jerks out there but hopefully most of the people in your life fall more into the fallible human category than the jerk category.

Did I learn all of this from one or two sessions in mandatory company-wide training? The concept was delivered there but it was concurrent with help from a very good friend. If we had a potential issue, since I was unable to validate my feelings and therefore also unable to own them, she'd do both of these things for me. Basically, she was my personal customer service agent.

For example, if she "misspoke," she was astute enough to see my emotional walls start to build and she'd quickly seek a conversation in which she'd explain her true meaning, enabling us to work through whatever the topic was. Had she not done this, I don't know that our friendship would have survived my emotional immaturity. Humbling as it is to say, she was essentially parenting me on validating my feelings.

For girls without daddies, validating and owning feelings can be like a chicken-and-egg situation – which comes first? On the one hand, you have to believe your feelings are valid in order to own them. On the other hand, you recognize your feelings stem from your unique circumstances, which might have been less than optimal, so by default you'll revert to questioning their validity.

None of that matters. You are who you are. Your feelings are valid, no matter what horrible circumstances might have predisposed you to having them. Accept them as valid and own them. Only then can you move on to the next levels of emotional maturity. You'll be pleasantly surprised how achieving the next levels will help your unique emotional reactions to evolve. But to get there you must first accept where you are now and own it.

7.

Making Others Like You

Possibly the scariest step in the path toward emotional maturity is the next level: emotional openness. Why is it scary? Up
to now we've been dealing with emotions internally. Emotional
openness involves exposing your emotions to others and potentially to the judgement of others. Why might girls without daddies
have a tougher struggle with this? How can they find the courage
to take this leap toward emotional maturity if they've tangled with
emotional openness in the past?

You're at a party. Someone starts talking to you. What's your
first thought? Is it to wonder what this person is like? Or is it,
"Will this person like me?" If it's the latter, there is a greater chance
you use defense mechanisms to protect yourself from the judgement of others and your emotional openness suffers as a result.

Controlling what feelings we disclose is a manipulative effort to
control how others respond to us and can be used as an attempt to
gain their approval.[1] Fear holds a person back from true connectivity with others because it keeps them from being honest about
how they really feel. How can one feel truly loved by another if
they aren't exposing their true feelings to the other person?

The factors inhibiting achievement of this level of emotional
responsibility aren't too different from the factors obstructing previous levels: unresolved past hurts, insecurity and lack of training[2],

to name a few. As noted in previous chapters, all of these will be more likely for girls without daddies.

Early in the development of a relationship, there's a cliff at whose edge you stand, the cliff of emotional openness. As you look down, you consider what happened the last time you stepped off. Was someone there to catch you or were the jagged rocks at the bottom the destiny that awaited you. Certainly, what happened the last time you stepped off is going to determine your answer. If it was painful, then insecurities likely resulted. Thus begins a cycle of hiding true emotions in an effort to protect your feelings, resulting in emotional isolation.

How do you step off the cliff when you expect to hit the jagged rocks at the bottom? It would certainly help if you could see someone you can count on waiting to catch you. Past hurts obstruct the view of whether someone safe is down there.

To get rid of those obstructions, you first have to deal with past hurts. That takes you back to the previous levels of emotional maturity – judgement causes pain; are you a victim? Validate and own your feelings.

A person must first be comfortable with her feelings before she can begin to express them to others. I'm not saying it's easy to go down memory lane and deal with past hurts. But life isn't meant to be easy, and how many things worth having didn't involve a lot of work?

At this point, let's ponder how girls without daddies might fare. Isn't it easier to see they might be inclined to select suboptimal romantic partners? They are less inclined to fear judgement from someone with obvious flaws than from someone who seems to have it all together. The unfortunate consequence of this selection is that it is also less likely to be a safe choice for emotional openness.

What happens next? New hurts and a tendency to emotionally close off, again. To avoid this cycle, my recommendation for girls without daddies is to first work through becoming emotionally open in friendships that involve less fear of rejection. In my opinion, that safer place is usually with female friends.

When I met my perfect friend, I didn't say much to anyone, let alone discuss my feelings. This friend initiated our friendship. She would call just to chat. She'd tell me about her day. I remembered wondering why she was telling me all these things. It wasn't that I didn't enjoy hearing about them but I marveled at her assumption that I would have any interest.

We began jogging together and she happened to mention that she wanted to run a marathon. Without much thought I said I'd join her. With that we began running regularly. When you run next to someone for many hours, eventually you need to fill the time with something. And that is how I began talking again. She had already taken the first step by exposing her emotions to me, thereby allowing me to feel safe disclosing personal things to her. Anytime I did share my feelings, they were always met with validation and acceptance. It was a smooth ride to emotional honesty with no setbacks.

At this point, already divorced from my young marriage and insecure about that failure, I mentioned to my jogging friend that it had cost me financially to get out of the marriage. Her answer was, "Some things are just worth paying for." I can quote that statement precisely because that one sentence had so much validation that it rang through my head repeatedly as I worked through accepting my failed marriage. Her response held no judgement, no inclination to perceive my divorce as my failure. Rather, she simply supported my decision to survive.

This was a safe training ground for the beginning of my emotional openness because it was as if I could see my friend at the bottom of that cliff with her arms out ready to catch me. When you begin your journey, recognize your beginner status and look for someone safe like this. If the person fails early on, consider setting them on the sidelines for a while as a candidate for catching you until you are strong enough to catch yourself. Ultimately, when you look over the edge of that cliff, the person you need to see down there with arms open is you.

Now let's consider an unsuccessful attempt at emotional openness. A woman has just begun dating a new guy. She has a bad day at work and calls to express her frustration to her new guy. His response is to try to solve her problems at work by suggesting how she might do things differently in the future.

If this woman is a girl without a daddy, she hears her feelings not being validated. She hears that she's brought her bad day on herself. She personalizes the man's response because she doesn't realize men typically tend to be fixers first and validators second. Why doesn't she realize that tendency? She didn't observe this type of exchange between her parents growing up.

On the other hand, if this woman is a girl with a daddy, she'll be strong enough to say to her new guy, "Listen, I appreciate what you're trying to do but I'm not asking you to solve my problems. I just want you to listen to me and say how much that sucks."

As I write this I laugh because only an emotionally mature guy could hear that and smile inside. I know this because I've tried it a few times. What do I do now if I've had a few bad things happen in one day and just want to give in to a moment of self-victimization? I call up a friend and tell them what I want. I start by saying I'm not looking for a fix here. My day just stank and I want someone to give me some sympathy. Most of my friends laugh and say, "Bring it on."

With that I've combined both the level of emotional openness and the next stage of emotional maturity, which is emotional assertiveness. I've asked for and received nurturing. We'll discuss this level in the next chapter.

When you've reached the beginning of emotional openness, you have two choices. Number one: protect yourself by hiding your true emotions from others in an effort to manipulate them into liking the false you. The result is emotional isolation. Choice number two: subject yourself to feelings of vulnerability by being emotionally open with those around you such that they truly know you.

Your reward for this risk is true emotional intimacy. If you don't try, you won't succeed.

8.

Do You Avoid Conflict?

The next level of emotional maturity is emotional assertiveness, the ability to ask for and receive nurturing. One step past disclosing our feelings, we are now asking for something in return. Unfortunately, when we are ready to ask for something we will likely be in a situation where we are not the only person with needs. In a romantic situation, this can easily lead to conflict.

As discussed, girls without daddies might tend to suppress their needs in favor of others, making the task of asserting them unfamiliar and daunting. The more likely outcome is conflict avoidance. How can girls without daddies face potential conflict and assert their emotional needs? This will be challenging because they have another disadvantage as they strive to achieve this new level of emotional maturity – they might be missing critical conflict management skills.

Let's first look at common conflict management styles and then identify which approaches are more likely to be used by girls without daddies:

- Accommodation/avoidance: Accommodation involves putting the interests of others ahead of your own. Avoidance means picking or not engaging in battles. Both of these styles often result in an undesirable outcome. When used excessively, both can result in self-victimization.

- Competition: A disruptive option where the goal is to win at all costs. I call this combative.

- Compromise: Second best, compromise is a style where some interests, but not all, are met.

- Collaboration: This is the preferred style, where everyone works together so everyone can win. Collaboration is a definite must for the toolbox and the one we would most often want to use.[1]

Although each style has times where its use might be warranted, in general the top two styles are the least desirable and the bottom two are the most desirable. Competition is rarely appropriate.

Which styles do girls without daddies tend to use most? They will lean toward accommodation/avoidance or competition as ways of managing interpersonal conflict. This tendency results from a higher prevalence of difficulties with both internalizing and externalizing behavior.[2]

Internalizing behavior problems manifests as self-victimization, which is reflective of accommodation and avoidance conflict management styles. Externalizing behavioral problems manifests in the use of the competitive, combative style.

As a child I preferred to be neither seen nor heard (accommodation/avoidance), whereas my sister believed in being both seen and heard (competitive/combative). She took on conflict after conflict. On one occasion, it ended up with her hiding between the piano and the piano bench as our stepfather hit and slapped at her. I was standing there. I did nothing. My mom was standing there. She did nothing. In fact, years later my sister and I discovered that our mother had completely blocked this entire event from her memory.

My poor sister made the mistake of constantly standing up for herself. It did not end well because she was using the same competitive style of conflict management as our stepfather, who also had to win at all costs. Had he used either of the more preferred styles to manage conflict, not only would these approaches have been taught to both my sister and me, but he and my sister would not have butted heads as much. In our house it was either self-silencing (accommodation) or all out warfare (competition).

Now let's consider which conflict management style girls with daddies might be more likely to use by looking at how they are influenced by a supportive father figure in the home. The most consistent styles of conflict management demonstrated by caring fathers are collaboration and accommodation.[3]

The use of accommodation by fathers always makes me chuckle as I think of the stereotypical father who makes peace with the neighbors by giving in to the neighbors' demands on things that only the wife cared about anyway. The difference between girls with and girls without daddies in this scenario is that girls with daddies have the example of collaboration, the most desirable style of conflict management, in their childhood homes. They're taught the essential skill of working through matters in a team environment so that everyone wins. Now that's a handy tool to have in one's toolbox.

Another influence on conflict management involves gender-based differences in communication styles. While women and men are both equally interested in a resolution, the styles employed differ in essential ways. In general, women tend to deal more with the context and detail of the conflict where as men lean more toward a "rational, linear and legalistic language."[4]

I've heard this described as women tending to paint a picture and then form a conclusion, while men reach a conclusion and then build support if needed. This is not a minor difference. I've seen many a man's eyes glaze over as women paint these pictures for them. Once when I was auditing a hospital the nurses were on strike. Management (at this time all men) was frustrated with the nurses' union negotiations because they felt the nurses (predominantly women at the time) couldn't prioritize their desires and, as a result, were unable to compromise on any point.

The gender specificity of communication styles indicates girls without daddies are likely to be oriented toward the picture style of communication, as their exposure to the typical male communication style will have been more limited. Impatience on the man's part can then develop. It will be more likely that a girl without a daddy will misinterpret this impatience as resistance to the negotiation when it could simply be the man's impatience with the communication style.

At this point, we've got a woman painting a picture and a man getting impatient. Add to that recipe a tendency for women to feel more vulnerable in conflicts in general due to concerns over identity and status and in particular more vulnerable in conflicts with men due to the physical dominance of the latter.[5]

This combination is likely to cause the woman to shift to accommodation – and down the rabbit hole we go for girls without daddies.

I learned the difference in communication styles between men and women not from my father but in the workplace. When I presented to senior executives or board members, typically men at that time, I quickly learned to start with the conclusion and then build support. If you want to see a competitive style of conflict management rear its ugly head, just scare the crap out of a board of directors by telling them how awful things could be before you first tell them everything is OK. One of these gentlemen actually helped me early on by asking why I didn't start at the end so it would be a lot easier to breathe through the rest of the information.

How can a girl without a daddy learn gender-specific communication styles and collaboration-oriented conflict management that will lead to resolution? Again, knowledge is the first step, and learning through trial and error is the second. When you are not successful, don't beat yourself up. Instead look for the learning opportunities. Review available conflict management styles. Remind yourself that you might tend to a less successful style and learn to develop signals in your feelings that tell you when this is happening so you can stop it.

Remember that communication styles between men and women can differ and try to adjust your presentation so that you're not adding unnecessary details and complications to the communication process.

Consider the following tips for achieving successful collaboration:

- Make sure you understand what the other person wants.

- Advocate for your own want without being critical of the other person's desires.

- Make sure that if the conversation gets emotional you wait until you can get it to feel safe for both parties before trying to resume meaningful conversation.

- Keep the conversation focused by not allowing other topics to take you off point.

- Develop a mutual purpose that gets things moving.

Make sure the collaboration ends in a meaningful outcome.[6, 7]

Ultimately my journey towards letting go of an accommodation style of conflict management was successful, but certainly that success was not immediate. At first, when I smelled any scent of conflict in the air, I found it difficult to stop the walls from creeping up around me. Yet I knew this bad habit had to be broken. Fortunately, I had read somewhere a habit only takes two to three weeks to break. Whether true or not, that tidbit gave me hope in my efforts to progress to more successful methods of conflict resolution.

It boiled down to putting the cart before the horse. I had to believe the person I was dealing with wanted collaboration even if my fear was telling me otherwise. I figured, "What's the harm?" If I didn't try I'd definitely not get a good collaborative result, so it seemed like the only thing at risk was my feelings.

As I transitioned from being conflict-averse to being a beginner at conflict resolution I had to accept that there was a learning curve, which inevitably involved interim failures. For example, the combination of my insecurities and my great desire not to enter into a conflict made me run hard at problems out of fear that if I wasn't running hard enough I'd stop short of addressing them.

This typically made for an accusatory opening to the conversation and headlong progression to conflict. Once I grew more comfortable that my position was valid and worth being heard, I could present my thoughts in a non-confrontational manner, which led to far more productive exchanges, often without any true conflict ever arising. My business training also helped me learn to be more linearly logical in my presentations. I was taught to always start with the bottom line and then fill in the details.

Many people avoid conflict. To this day I strongly dislike the noise and angst that accompany discord and I suspect that was inherent in my nature regardless of my home life as a child. Nonetheless, I have learned that some battles are worth fighting, including battles for my own self-interests.

At this point in my life, I look at any dispute and assess whether it is part of a pattern or just a single incident. If it is a single incident in an established healthy relationship, I'm likely to call it a fluke and look the other way. It just depends on the topic and whether I can really emotionally let go of what was said or done.

But if it is a new relationship or a situation that could develop into a negative pattern, I'm more likely to have a chat with the person and discuss the matter. Now that I am comfortable with my ability to assess situations and know that I deserve to be treated fairly, this type of discussion rarely involves conflict. I merely make inquiries about what happened and present my position on the matter, seeking understanding from the other party and working towards a mutually satisfactory conclusion.

Another word of caution – patterns of behavior do not change overnight. Just because you have a meeting of the minds doesn't mean that the other person's old behaviors won't rear their ugly heads again in the future. Don't interpret a slip in the other person's behavior to be an assault on your self-worth and fall back into acceptance of a situation you are unhappy about. When attempting to change a pattern of behavior in a salvageable relationship, you might need to have the conversation a few times. Try to remain confident in the worthiness of your request and readdress the matter as many times as is necessary.

Emotional maturity is within the grasp of girls without daddies. Taking a step toward that maturity will require an understanding of the differences between how men and women communicate and learning the preferred methods of conflict management. By being an effective communicator you can avoid conflict without practicing conflict avoidance. In doing so, you are more likely to be successful in asserting your needs for emotional nurturing.

9.

Do You Feel Worthless?

The next level of emotional maturity is emotional understanding. At this level, a person realizes that self-concepts are the problem, because all self-concepts have both good and bad sides. One side cannot exist without the other.[1] We will look at common self-concepts in this chapter and the next. The first is one that involves feelings of worth versus worthlessness.

Here again, parenting is key. If a child receives positive reinforcement, she is more likely to feel worthy. In stark contrast, a child heavily criticized by parental figures, or who observed parents criticizing themselves, is likely to suffer from feelings of worthlessness.[2]

At this point it probably goes without saying that girls without daddies are more likely to be subject to suboptimal parenting, leaving them more likely to feel unimportant. When a person is not conscious of these feelings of worthlessness, the challenge can be even greater, as it's difficult to battle an enemy you don't know exists.

I was not consciously aware of my feelings of worthlessness until the moment I became startlingly aware of them. Early in my professional career, while working as an auditor, I was assigned to interview the Chief Financial Officer of a publicly traded company. It was a simple auditor interview about subsequent events, something an auditor with my level of experience should be able to handle easily.

But I had seen the guy I was going to interview in action. He was, and in my opinion continues to be, one of the most brilliant people I have ever met. During the interview he was kind, though he could surely see how nervous I was. As I walked away from the interview, I remember thinking that I'd gone further in my career than I should have. I remember feeling that I had no business meeting with a professional of that caliber on my own.

I was stunned at this negative impression I had of myself. I knew I was smart. Why would I ever think so little of myself? If the situation had not been so extreme, I probably would never have noticed the disparity between these feelings about myself versus my intellectual impression of myself. I thought about it a long time, and ultimately I tied my reaction to an unresolved incident in my childhood.

Many years ago, I had read about this type of incident involving children described as "casting a spell." The spell cast on me had a lasting impact but had been so internalized that I had never even realized it until that interview.

Here is the story of witchcraft.

When I was twelve years old we went to the Pendleton Roundup in eastern Oregon, a well-known rodeo in the Pacific Northwest. On this trip were my mother and stepfather, my sister and me and two other families with children.

One day we all went to lunch in the hotel restaurant. The only available seating was at the counter. It was like musical chairs – and guess who ended up without a chair? Me. I made what turned out to be a horrible decision to step between my mother and stepfather at their counter seats to say I didn't have a place to sit. My stepfather was in peak form and loudly barked out that not only did he not care whether I got a seat, he didn't even care if I got to eat.

Before I go into how this affected me, let's stop for a minute and consider how this might have played out if that little girl had a loving father sitting amongst the others at that restaurant counter and some other adult had spoken to his daughter that way. I'm quite certain that little girl would have had a seat and I wonder what seat the offender would be on.

Back to the girl without a daddy in the restaurant that day. I was stunned. Everyone looked at me. In my memory, even the waitress at the counter was looking at me. I felt so small. I turned and left the restaurant. No one followed me. I made my second mistake. Having no key to our hotel room, I walked around and ended up in a store by the hotel. It looked like one of those membership stores, so I wasn't sure whether I could go in. After being shunned at the restaurant, I was too afraid to ask.

Instead, I stood there between the door and the counter pondering what to do. I could see people watching me. Having just had this spell of unworthiness cast upon me, I was sure they were wondering why I thought I had a right to be there. Of course, I now know they were probably worried about me. At twelve years old I looked only nine at best, being quite small. Later when I rejoined "my" group there was no discussion of the incident. We just moved forward, going to the rodeo, swimming in the pool and eating. The situation was never discussed further.

The spell had been cast. Any impression I had that I mattered was shattered that day in the restaurant. There is a book that speaks to this concept, *The Transcendent Child: Tales of Triumph over the Past*, by Lillian B. Rubin. The book discusses how a child can survive an unsupportive home life. While my childhood life was not nearly as rough as some described, one of the primary concepts in the book is that some children survive because they don't believe they deserve better. When I was reading the book I had not yet recognized the spell that had been cast on me. I remember chuckling at the idea that I was resilient in my youth simply because I didn't think I deserved more, but as it turns out that was in fact the case.

I had excused my father's absence to spare myself pain. I had excused my mother's tendency to defer to men, including my step-father, because I knew she just wasn't strong enough to stand up to them. If I had been my sister, I would have been pained constantly by these things because I would have known I deserved better.

My sister always struggled with the absence of our father because she apparently knew fathers had roles and also knew our dad was flaking out on his. She wasn't what the book described as transcendent. She lived in the same home as me but really didn't survive it well at all. She fought everyone and everything because she believed she deserved better. It turns out that in her own way she was stronger than me because she never accepted that she deserved so little.

I was shocked to realize that, at the expense of my self-esteem, I had ignored the pain of what had happened to me that day in the restaurant. I had long ago negatively adjusted my self-perception to be able to survive. I thought I was a strong, independent woman. In reality, I was a hurt little girl. It is no wonder that when I initially read the concept of a transcendent child I had dismissed it. It was too painful. It took the conflict between my presumed self-image and what the little voice inside me whispered after that interview with the Chief Financial Officer to make me see reality.

Obviously, no one deserves to be belittled like I was as a little girl that day in Pendleton, Oregon. It wasn't until I was in my thirties that I figured out why no one said anything on that awful day.

I was returning pop cans to the grocery store – in Oregon you pay a small deposit and get the money back when you return the cans. The young man counting the cans was mentally challenged and was moving slowly. Quite a line was building up but we all seemed content to wait our turn. If the others were thinking the same as me, they were thinking how wonderful it was that this mentally challenged young man had been given this opportunity for employment by this big grocery store chain.

Suddenly, a loud young female employee arrived and began berating the male employee in front of us as she ripped cans out of his hands and began throwing them about. Among other derogatory comments, she repeatedly told the young man he was stupid. All of us, about five adult customers, stood there with our mouths wide open. None of us spoke.

I walked away ashamed. I couldn't believe it. Even though I had excused the adults in the restaurant when I was a little girl, I always thought I would behave differently. Yet when my turn came to stand up for what was right, I stood there silently just like those adults in the restaurant.

They weren't silent because I was worthless. More likely, the "bystander effect" came into play. Studies indicate that the greater the number of people that observe such instances, the less likely they are to intervene. One reason for inaction is the simple diffusion of responsibility. Another is pluralistic ignorance, the thought that it must not be that bad if no one else is reacting.[3]

My inaction after seeing the young man ridiculed was a combination of both.

After I had walked away, my sense of justice burst out. I sought out the store manager to complain about this horrible incident. He assured me that the young man was new and would improve. But he had misunderstood me. He thought I was upset about getting slow service from the young man. I began sobbing and blubbered that it wasn't the young man I was upset with, it was the young woman. I told the manager how awful the young woman had treated the young man, and concluded by threatening that if I ever saw her in the store again, it would be the last time I shopped there. The manager was shocked, but I never saw that young woman in the store again.

I'm sure the manager had no idea why I had such a strong emotional reaction. Sure, I was upset about what I had just witnessed, but the outburst of sobbing was the little girl in me finally realizing what had happened long ago in Pendleton. And it was me realizing that I was no better than the adults in that restaurant. It was me finally understanding why they just sat there. I had assumed all those adults were silent because they agreed I wasn't important enough for them to adjust their lunch plans. In reality I was looking at the faces of shocked adults who were all probably waiting on one another to speak up.

There is a television show about this, *What Would You Do?* I've watched it a couple of times. They plant people in public places and create scenes where these actors behave inappropriately to see if any bystanders will speak up against what is happening. In the episodes I watched no one pointed out that the silence of some of the witnesses is part of the sociological phenomenon of group functioning. Perhaps the producers pursued it later as the show evolved. I hope so.

It may sound a bit obvious to say that I'd like to be the woman I am now in the body of that little girl in the restaurant. After hearing the mean words of my stepfather, whom I would now whisk out of my life as unworthy of my friendship, instead of walking away silently, I would politely but confidently say, "Sir, I was not speaking to you. I was speaking to my mother." That would have been enough to break through that social barrier of silence and any number of adults might have offered me their seat provided I wasn't knocked on my butt for speaking out against my stepfather. But that's another story.

As it stands now, I have only a smile on my face when I relive that event, armed now with a clearer perspective. As for lifting the spell cast on me, I used a counter-spell for a while until that negative little voice in my head no longer could be heard. The counter spell was simply positive self-talk. Now that I was sensitized to recognizing when that negative little voice was speaking silently but still yelling at me, I'd battle it with my own audible positive self-talk. Whatever negativity had been built in me, I'd counter it by simply telling myself the opposite.

For example, in the case of not feeling worthy of interviewing the Chief Financial Officer, I talked out loud to myself, preferably someplace private so as not to appear insane, and tell myself, "You know you are smart. You know you are worthy. You are a kind, caring person deserving of good things." The specific words are not important. What's important is that you counter this latent negativity that's built into your processing by overpowering it with affirmations.

Positive self-talk is one of the most commonly recommended approaches for dealing with feelings of worthlessness.

"When we do not see worth in something, we often treat it poorly. Self-worth is the same way," according to Brooke Lewis, a registered clinical counselor who specializes in self-harm, eating disorders and addictions in British Columbia. You truly believe you aren't "worth caring for."

According to Lewis, people with a low self-worth find it challenging to speak kindly to themselves. She suggests collecting inspirational quotes online, saving them to your phone and then

reading them throughout the day. This teaches you how to gener-
ate positive self-talk, so that over time, you might start making
similar kind statements to yourself. These statements, she said,
can be anything that helps to soothe and reassure you, such as "It's
going to be OK," and, "You did your best."[4]

After recognizing my feelings of worthlessness, did I break
free of them? I'm happy to say that years later I became the Chief
Financial Officer of a publicly traded company, in the same position as that brilliant man I had interviewed when I identified
my self-limiting thoughts! I had discovered the opposite side of
worthlessness – worthiness.

Being cognizant of both, and realizing both exist, I'm closer to
emotional understanding.

10.

Do You Feel Like a Failure?

Continuing our path to emotional understanding, we will look at another self-concept that has both positives and negatives – feeling like a failure or a success. Feeling like a success can occur only after we limit feelings of failure. Feeling like a failure occurs when we internalize past failures and incorporate them into our concept of who we are as a person. Are girls without daddies pre-disposed by their background to the negative internalization of feelings of failure as compared to girls with daddies? If so, how do they remedy this negative self-concept?

Feelings of failure are a result of low self-esteem. A Queendom study found that people with low self-esteem scored higher on perfectionism scores than people with high self-esteem. In addition, those with low self-esteem were often more disappointed in others around them.[1]

Put another way, low self-esteem drives us to perfectionistic tendencies. A sick twist of fate is that no one can be perfect and therefore our failures only serve to further damage our self-esteem. In addition, they strain our relationships with those around us because we hold them to unrealistically high standards.

With regard to the differences on this point between girls with and without daddies, research finds that "...women's perception of their father's unconditional regard was significantly related to

self-esteem, whereas their perception of their mother's unconditional regard was only weakly related to self-esteem."[2] Thus, girls
with supportive fathers are more likely to have higher self-esteem
and are less likely to be hounded by feelings of failure.

I was the classic example of a perfectionist hounded by feelings
of failure. To become emotionally aware on this point, I went back
to those videos in my head. My infamous stepfather had a multitude of rules, and failure to comply strictly with those rules did
not yield a positive experience - not exactly an environment ooz-
ing with unconditional regard. Don't get me wrong, I had people
in my life that believed in me and were positive influences. Yet
the dominance of negative reinforcement from my stepfather over-
powered the positives.

Having a burned-in need to be perfect wasn't all bad. Its happy
side-effect was a desire to excel and succeed at whatever I put my
mind to. I expected myself to get straight A's in school. I expected
myself to be excellent at work. That's the good news. One bad side
effect was that the inevitable failures were hard for me to swallow.
My stepfather's intolerance of my imperfections became my own.

Any mistake I made was gut-wrenching. Ultimately, my over-
sensitivity to my own simple human failings became counterproductive. It began to hinder personal growth rather than propel it.

Let me give an example of this counterproductive tendency.
Many years ago we had a terrible snow storm in our area. We
were under three feet of snow with an inch of freezing rain on
top of that. Unfortunately, I had made a terrible mistake during
the storm. I own a small ranch with horses. My barn was full so
I decided to move all my pregnant mares into my indoor arena
to get them off the snow and ice. I thought I was doing the right
thing. How could they be left outside?

On Christmas Eve, the weather started to warm and the snow began to melt. The snow on my barn slid down and rested up against a slant that joined the arena to the barn. The arena apparently was not built for that type of lateral pressure and at about 11:00 p.m. on Christmas Eve there was a horrible sound. I ran out to discover that a portion of my arena had collapsed. Tragically, it was the area covering the temporary stalls for my pregnant mares.

I dug quickly through the metal and snow, fearing that the horses were suffering. They were not. They had been killed instantly. The emergency people I got on the phone advised me to get out of the arena, which I promptly did. I heard more sounds and watched as the rest of the arena imploded.

Under any circumstances this would have been horrible, but I made it even worse because I couldn't accept that I had made the mistake that cost those horses their lives. Yes, my arena had been a sound and well-built structure. Yes, buildings collapsed all over the area. Yes, the area was declared a natural disaster and FEMA came in to help. Regardless, I tortured myself for not anticipating the collapse of my arena. I took something awful and made it even worse by punishing myself.

My habit of internalizing negative self-talk was in play. Instead of my stepfather listing all the reasons I wasn't good enough, I took the task upon myself. Did my perfectionism stop with judging my own shortcomings? No, it didn't. My insecurities became veiled in my judgements of others.

It's hard for me to consider that I might have been hard on others in an attempt to build myself up, as that would, of course, mean another form of failure. Yet it wasn't until I was comfortable with myself that I could much more easily accept the shortcomings of others. Consider this tendency in light of the chapter "Judgement Causes Pain." It is a self-fulfilling downward spiral

– low self-esteem, perfectionist tendencies, judging the inadequacies of others, causing our own pain.

Addressing my perfectionistic tendencies was difficult because it was really a side-effect of my low self-esteem. I realized I had assimilated my stepfather's role of punishing me for my alleged failures. It was tough for me to acknowledge that I had internalized one of the behaviors I resented most in my stepfather.

So I decided that from now on I would be the person that should have been there when I made a mistake. I decided to be that loving father that tells his daughter it's OK when she makes a mistake. When I realized I was being hard on myself, I'd actually talk to myself – again, trying not to do so in a manner that made me look weird to bystanders. I told myself, "You're not perfect. No one is perfect. You were never meant to be perfect. It's OK that you made a mistake."

I should note here that I later learned that affirmations should be positive, but these semi-positive affirmations worked for me at the time. I would repeat them until I could finally accept them. Eventually, I was able to leave this tool behind because I had replaced the previous negative programming with new positive programming.

Emotional understanding requires an investigation of the forces that determine who we have become. This can often be painful. Realizing that my perfectionistic needs were a function of low self-esteem allowed me to address the core problem and grow. Instead of failure consuming me, I saw it as a fruitful learning opportunity. Some of the best things in my life have come out of my greatest failures. If I could not accept that I may have made a mistake and look at it with honest open eyes, it would have been impossible to move on and look for the learning value of those mistakes. Life is a journey full of missteps.

Emotional understanding is now one step closer because yet another self-concept, feeling like a failure/success, has been acknowledged. It is understood that both must exist and that both have value. Certainly other self-concepts will require pursuit – unhappy/content, anxious/calm, impatient/patient, negative/positive, external motivation/internal motivation.

Moving forward on this path of enlightenment will require you to pay attention to those subtle negative voices in your head, seek an understanding of where they come from, and reprogram those voices so you see the targeted self-concept as having a positive side as well as the negative side on which you might be focused. Once accomplished, the ability to move on to the next level of emotional maturity is possible – emotional detachment.

11.

Finally, Emotional Maturity

The last level of emotional maturity is emotional detachment. Ah, that beautiful time when you are aware of and content with who you are, such that no one can rip that sense of wellbeing out of your hands. With emotional understanding, you quit measuring yourself against outside factors but rather look inward, and when you look inward you accept that there's going to be both good and bad aspects to your self-concepts. Emotional detachment occurs when you let go of all self-concepts, have nothing to defend or promote, and are therefore freed to love unconditionally.[1]

I always think of the achievement of emotional detachment like riding a bike or learning to downhill ski. It's tough to explain but once you do it you understand and you'll never forget how to do it.

For me emotional detachment came after I retired. I'd been a successful senior executive for a large company. I went from walking into a room as the person people both feared and wanted to impress (or so I thought) to being nobody (or so I thought). For a while, I missed all the acclaim that was served up with my success. I was stuck with both the outside perspective of who I was and my internal self-concept.

For a while I felt the need to explain that I'd been successful, that I really was somebody. Then at one point I just let go of it. I told the person pushing my two-wheeled bike to let go and off I went, free as a bird, and I never went back. I ceased caring whether other people thought I was anybody special and I accepted that I was both a success and retired. I found peace within myself by not defining myself at all. I was neither a success nor a failure. I was me.

How do you know when you've arrived? You will know because you will have the feeling I just described, emotional freedom. If you are setting a path toward emotional maturity, here are the characteristics that you seek:

- Being secure enough to be vulnerable and therefore able to both give and receive love.

- The ability to face problems and deal with them promptly.

- The ability to view life as an experience, enjoy success, accept responsibility of failure and learn from it.

- The ability to accept frustration and move forward.

- The ability to handle hostility constructively.

- The ability to exist in relaxed confidence knowing you are able to get what you want from life.[2]

It is my hope that when you get to the chapter on setting goals you put emotional maturity down as a goal that you believe is achievable and that you are motivated to seek.

12.

Your Type of Guy

What type of guy do you find yourself attracted to? There is a great book that goes deeply into this topic titled *Women who Love too Much* by Robin Norwood. I recommend this book for women who had fathers that were physically or emotionally abusive or fathers addicted to drugs or alcohol. The book discusses how women can confuse familiarity with feelings of love.

Girls with loving and supportive father figures have the distinct advantage of being more likely to fall in love with a loving and supportive man. Girls with what I call the anti-daddy are more likely to be initially attracted to anti-men, which could include alcoholic or physically abusive partners. Couple that with the fact that breaking up is hard to do for girls without caring father figures and you've got a recipe for disaster.

What type of guy will girls without daddies seek when they lacked even an anti-daddy? I compared this tendency to pick the familiar with my own youthful romantic choices. My available selections were an anti-daddy, an absent daddy, and the abyss. It would seem natural that I'd lean toward the most familiar or dominant father figure, which would be my stepfather. But, that wasn't the case. I didn't pick anyone like him. Of course, he wasn't my biological father. Perhaps that differentiation allowed me to break the pattern. In looking at my dating relationships, I'd say

I wasn't doing the selecting at all. I was more the recipient of the selection process. Regardless, selection was not my core problem, my insecurities were.

Let's say a girl without a daddy happens to selects a truly wonderful guy. Her chances of damaging that relationship, even though this theoretical guy is perfect, are still pretty darn high. Why? There are several factors.

A girl without a daddy is going to be less familiar with how to handle a relationship with a man because she never had simulated experiences with her own father. She's never seen the balancing of power in a relationship by observing it in her parents' marriage. A girl without a daddy is simply going into this relationship with an empty toolbox. Given that she's dating Mr. Wonderful, she still has a chance, but even Mr. Wonderful is human and that will undoubtedly lead to bumps in the road that a girl without a daddy might not be prepared to handle.

As already discussed, a girl without a caring father is also more likely to have lower self-confidence, which is particularly true when it comes to Mr. Wonderful. How will it be possible for a person with low self-esteem to maintain a balanced relationship with anyone, let alone Mr. Wonderful? He would have to be godlike to be able to maintain the balance for both of them – not impossible, but the odds are not good. So what is the point? Sadly, the truth is that until you've resolved the issues your fatherless childhood burdened you with your chances of a successful romantic relationship are not great. As a reminder, "Daughters who live in mother-only homes are 92% more likely to divorce."[1]

Further support for this conclusion comes from research that identifies several behavior patterns that fatherless women may follow:

- Promiscuity. Without having a father to reinforce her self-worth she may encounter difficulty relating to men because of unconscious efforts to seek approval. This path may lead to multiple sexual relationships where, in the woman's eyes, sex equals love. This path of promiscuity, however, only weakens her self-worth.

- Marrying daddy. Falling in love with an older man may provide a replicated father figure. This works as long as the man is comfortable with the woman eventually achieving a sense of her self-worth. If the man is not, he might feel threatened by her emotional growth and begin some form of psychological abuse, which again begins to undermine her evolving wholeness.

- Not engaging emotionally. This can take the form of staying single, perhaps as part of dedication to career, or not engaging emotionally in relationships, possibly through prostitution or only dating unavailable/married men.[2]

Let's start with promiscuity. Having had a rather proper mother, I personally didn't take this approach, but it would have been easy to go down this road, particularly if I had observed my mom dating men regularly in my youth. However, I've observed this tendency in many female friends who were fatherless. Statistics also indicate that fatherless women are more prone to earlier sexual experiences:

- A study using a sample of 1,409 rural southern adolescents, 851 females and 558 males aged 11-18 years, investigated the correlation between father absence and self-reported sexual activity. The results revealed that adolescents in father-absence homes were more likely to report being sexually active compared to adolescents living with their fathers.[3]

- Being raised by a single mother raises the risk of teen pregnancy.

- Children from single parent families are twice as likely to enter into early sexual activity.

From all these statistics it isn't a far reach to see that girls without daddies are more predisposed to head down the debilitating path of promiscuity. There are two important points on the issue of looking for love through sex. First, you are likely to damage your self-esteem through these failed attempts to find love. Second, men and women view sex very differently. We discuss this perspective further in the next chapter.

In terms of marrying daddy, aside from strapping yourself to someone who might be wearing Depends in a few years, there's a good chance, as noted above, that under his protection you will mature, which may cause him to become insecure and possibly abusive to maintain control of the relationship. In such a case, the fix is short-lived and you may soon find yourself in a worse place than where you started. Although my choices weren't for an older man, this was still my category of choice. I looked for a protector/rescuer. The results fit the stereotypical risk perfectly. It ended because as I matured my partner became emotionally abusive.

As for being emotionally absent from relationships, there's no great need to discuss the negatives of prostitution or of restricting yourself to relationships with unavailable men. Obviously, the important goal is to recognize why you might have this tendency and address the core problem so that you can find either a satisfying long-term romantic relationship, or at least not put yourself in potentially harmful or dangerous relationships such as those that involve prostitution or adultery.

If you are a girl without a daddy, this has probably been a pretty depressing chapter. Don't despair. The reality is that once you realize you yourself have to be whole in order to be half of a relationship, you have taken the first step toward eventually forming a successful romantic bond.

Remember that familiarity does not equal love, that sex won't buy you love, and that hiding won't find you love. When you meet a potential romantic interest, you don't want your first thought to be whether he likes you. The goal is to get to where your first thought is whether he is worthy of you.

13.

Using Sex to Get Your Man

When it comes to understanding the meaning of sex to men and women, girls without daddies have a training deficit that deepens this labyrinth, making it nearly impossible to navigate. If you are a girl without a daddy, recognizing this difference is critical to either stopping or preventing a disabling behavior pattern – using sex to get your man – and the resulting downward spiral of your self-respect.

The confusion around this topic starts with the difference between how men and women view sex, regardless of whether the women grew up with a supportive father figure. In the book *His Needs, Her Needs*, William F. Harley describes the top ten needs of men and women and concludes that they are largely the same. However, the top five for men are completely different from the top five for women. Put bluntly, sex is in the top five needs for men and in the top ten for women, but not the top five. This difference in prioritization can be challenging for all relationships, but for girls without daddies it is much more than a challenge, it is a minefield.

Imagine a little girl with a loving father figure. As she grows up, he tells her that she's beautiful and that any man should consider it an honor and a privilege to be selected by her as a husband. That little girl is more likely to carefully assess the men she dates. She's going to keep her physicality as a precious gift that is only to be given to someone worthy of her.

Now imagine a little girl growing up without a loving father figure in her life. She still yearns for that male approval and validation of her beauty and worthiness. She wants a man's approval, love and devotion. When this little girl grows up, she is much more likely to confuse physical attention from a man for the validation, love and devotion she has been seeking.

She hasn't had those conversations with a loving father figure who explains that men might place less emotional attachment to the act of sex than women do. He might even mention the alleged belief that men think about sex more frequently than can be counted. In short, a girl without a supportive father figure hasn't been taught that a man's physical attention doesn't necessarily hold the emotional context she might ascribe to it.

This second little girl is much more likely to pursue physical intimacy because she believes that it means her male suitor loves her.[1] She might even be the initiator of sex in an effort to capture her man's love through physical intimacy. This grand canyon of expectations between what she seeks and what she might get can only serve to damage her already poor self-esteem, leading her to continue this damaging pattern of seeking a man's affection through serial sexual relationships.

Here's a story from a male friend of mine who started dating a young woman. He explained that after a couple of dates he had sex with her because it was late, they'd been making out and he felt she would have been disappointed had he not. I can only guess that she thought that if this kind man had sex with her it would mean something huge. It did not. I believe that was their last date.

This man did not set out to do this but when offered the temptation he certainly wasn't able to walk away. The woman might have given something important, thinking it held great meaning. From the man's point of view, he was doing her a courtesy by avoiding rejecting her. Believe it or not, this man was a nice guy. I just can't say it enough – for girls without daddies sex holds meanings of affirmation and devotion but for most men that is not necessarily the case.

My own example is fairly harmless. As a young adult I was in an on-again, off-again relationship – it was so hard to really break up with a guy back then. In my mind, if we were physically intimate, meaning in my case just kissing, it meant the man had feelings for me. I would seek opportunities for a make-out session with him because I needed the affirmation I believed it indicated. In this case, I was giving the person at least part of what he wanted and I was getting the affection I so badly desired. In terms of his needs/her needs, it was almost a win/win.

Regardless, the key point is that in a man's mind a kiss can be just a kiss, whereas in the mind of a girl without a daddy that is not necessarily the case. Looking back, I can easily see that my efforts were hopeless as well as ineffectively manipulative. Fortunately, my mother's model of prudishness saved me from developing a damaging habit beyond this level of intimacy.

It is easy to see how a parental example of promiscuity, coupled with the need for affection, could easily have led down the destructive path of seeking emotional intimacy through sex. The more likely outcome is disappointment at best and the inevitable forfeiting of dignity and self-respect.

A girl without a daddy might even be the initiator of sex in an effort to capture her man's love through physical intimacy. This grand canyon of expectations between what she seeks and what she might get can only serve to damage her already poor self-esteem, leading her to continue this damaging pattern of seeking a man's affection through sexual relationship after sexual relationship.

Relevant statistics on this topic are:

- A British study found that girls brought up by lone parents were twice as likely to leave home by age 18 as the daughters of intact homes; were three times as likely to be cohabiting by age 20; and almost three times as likely to have a birth out of wedlock.[2]

- As sociologist David Blankenhorn puts it, "If the evidence suggests that fatherless boys tend toward disorderly and violent behavior, it just as clearly suggests that fatherless girls tend toward personally and socially destructive relationships with men, including precocious sexual activity and unmarried motherhood.[3]

- Females who lose their father figures to divorce or abandonment seek much more attention from men and had more physical contact with boys their age than girls from intact homes....These females constantly seek refuge for their missing father and as a result there is a constant need to be accepted by men from whom they aggressively seek attention (Bogan and Krohn[1]).

Don't get me wrong. There are a lot of great guys out there that hold to the same standards of physical intimacy as many women. But there are plenty that don't. If you are a woman without a loving father figure in your life, it will be important for you to understand that you are vulnerable to the physical advances of men because you might attach undue significance to those advances.

Don't give more than you want to. Don't give expecting to get something in return. Give only what you truly want, so you don't get your heart broken because sex meant something to you, yet to the guy in your life it was only sex.

Personally, I believe that casual sexual encounters are dangerous from many perspectives, not least of which is the danger of sexually transmitted diseases. Regardless of my own beliefs, I suggest waiting as long as possible before becoming physically intimate for several reasons. First, you don't want to use sexuality as a trap. Not only is it most likely ineffective for reasons discussed above, but even in the best scenario for a girl without a daddy the relationship will probably become unbalanced because sex may mean more to the girl.

This imbalance can affect your behavior, resulting in insecurities, clinginess, jealousy and a myriad other outcomes simply because you might not be whole enough to give so much in a romantic relationship.

Equally important, advancing a relationship to a sexual level will make leaving that relationship more difficult, particularly for girls without daddies because they have a tougher time moving on. This difficulty can be more intense once sex is involved because self-worth is tied up in believing the relationship was valid. You won't want to see yourself as having been easy or taken advantage of. And finally, if you are attracted to unhealthy relationships, you might find yourself in an abusive situation that has advanced to physical intimacy. This will only serve to escalate the state of affairs beyond your control and make your ability to extricate yourself even more difficult.

It might be old-fashioned to believe that a respectful man will honor the woman he loves and never ask her to do something that does not help her maintain a healthy self-esteem. A lot of baggage comes with previous sexual encounters and therefore it would be wonderful if all that noise could be eliminated at the beginning of a fantastic life-long romantic relationship. For all girls, but particularly for girls without daddies, I believe abstinence for as long as possible is a healthier avenue. And I'll bet there are many loving, supportive father figures out there that would agree with me.

If you've already had sex with your significant other do not despair. Every day is a new day and every step we take helps us learn so that the next step we take can head us in the long-term direction we want to go. The point is not to make you feel bad about previous decisions. The goal is to point out behavioral patterns that might not be healthy in the long run so you can examine them and consider making the changes you deem appropriate.

My strong suggestion is that you do not try to use sex to capture your man. Even if you manage to throw the fish back in, you're still left with the emotional consequences. Conversely, you could end up feeling like you were the fish that was tugged on and then thrown back after being caught. If you are a girl without a daddy you simply might not yet have the proper toolbox to be making decisions about physical intimacy.

14.

Can Men Be Just Friends?

As a former manager, I often contemplated whether a boss and an employee could be friends without the employee taking advantage of the familiarity. A much more relevant question that I should have been considering is whether or not men and women can be just friends. We'll begin looking at this topic regardless of whether the women had supportive father figures.

Let's first consider what research indicates:

- The study suggests that women generally think guys and gals can 'just be friends,' while men are secretly hoping there's a chance their relationships with their female friends can be something more. Basically, this study gives us the scientific explanation for the 'friend zone.' Women and men are often on completely different wavelengths when it comes to their cross-sex relationships![1]

- Men and women may sometimes have very different goals and desires in opposite-sex friendships. Although both may sometimes be looking for a companion and nothing more, on other occasions, plans may differ. More specifically, men appear to be more likely to look at opposite sex friends as potential sexual and romantic partners. Women, in contrast, tend to prefer non-sexual friendships, which provide protection and resources.[2]

Of course, every situation will vary and there are certainly times when cross-sex friendships can work out just fine. Regardless, we cannot ignore that case studies indicate more often than not there might be different expectations from a cross-sex friendship for the men and women involved.

Now let's make the situation a little more complicated by restricting the females to girls without daddies. Given that women in general might be looking more for protection and resources, how much more so would a girl without a daddy aim for this? Then add lower self-esteem and fear of rejection and imagine her warding off romantic advances from her "friend." Of course, she finds rejecting this man difficult so she succumbs to his advances. Then throw on top of that mess the difficulty she will have leaving relationships. I've likely just described either a life of mediocrity or a pending relationship disaster.

At one point in my life I actually began to wonder whether I was sending mixed signals to male friends, including married male friends. On more than one occasion I found myself the recipient of romantic advances from males I thought were firmly in the "just friends" category.

Unfortunately, because I was satisfied with the benefits of the friendship I had not considered whether the same was true for my male friends. The man's ultimate revelation of his true feelings was usually accompanied by either a verbal or physical romantic advance leaving me a hopeless choice between forcing feelings that didn't exist or facing the almost certain loss of my dear (male) friend and the unwanted rejection of me that would imply.

Was I at fault? Ultimately, I concluded I was not. Amusingly, at the beginning of my soul searching, I discussed this dilemma with a male acquaintance (a casual friend) and that man laughed out loud. He said the only mistake I had made was assuming that men can be just friends. I doubt he had even read the research!

Also, I've had several female friends who had supportive father figures who found themselves in this same situation, so I know the occurrence is not unique to me or other girls without daddies. However, I think the outcome might have been more painful to me than it was to my friends with supportive father figures. I leaned on my male friendships with a sort of surrogate father-figure familiarity. Combine that familiarity with the male tendency to hope for more than friendship and voila, there's now an inevitable finish to the friendship that my ignorance had obscured.

My only wish is that I had evolved past my fatherless tendencies earlier so that I could have avoided the repeated devastating loss of close friends because I simply could not reciprocate their romantic feelings. I would have chosen my male friends differently. Certainly, none of them would have included married men in unhealthy marriages. I would have made my wish for only friendship explicitly clear such that if they were only in the friendship with hopes for romance they would have ditched me earlier. It would have been less painful.

Don't get me wrong. I believe men and women can be just friends because I have had several close male friendships that never crossed this boundary. Nonetheless, this potential is something girls without daddies should be keenly aware of, particularly if they are looking to their male friends for a type of emotional support that might cause confusion.

A further complication is the "older man" syndrome. In chapter 12 we discussed the concept of marrying daddy. Unless daddy has kept himself in damn good physical shape, what do you bet these relationships started with a cross-sex surrogate father -figure friend-zone relationship that was pushed by surrogate daddy to be something more? In my view, this is more likely with men over 50, as they seem to view themselves as rescuers, which has the unhappy side-effect of prolonging women's fruitless tendencies to see them as such. Of course, these generalities are unfair to the more evolved of the male species.

All that being said, I truly found no difference in a man's level of confusion over friendship versus romance based solely on the man's age. But there was definitely a difference on my part. When I (unknowingly) used an older man in a friendship as a surrogate father figure, which meant they were not of romantic interest to me, I was less vigilant as the idea of a romantic development seemed far from plausible. In such friendships I would lean on them like a father, confide in them, look to their opinions and seek their approval as I would with a father.

What I didn't realize was that sometimes these men did not view the friendship in the same manner. If these men made unwanted advances I found it hurtful because I felt deceived. My disappointment was palpable when I realized what I thought was fatherly friendship was a façade for something more. We can conclude with this point by using the old adage "buyer beware." You might think you are getting a friend by what you are pulling off the shelf is a whole lot of something else.

This chapter is a warning more than anything else. Be aware that your toolbox for dealing with these situations is probably not up to the job of dealing with potentially troublesome friendship complexities. Emotionally intimate relationships that have zero sexual context will be easier for a girl looking for a surrogate father figure, but that doesn't mean that the man will be able to differentiate between that emotional intimacy and a progression toward a physically intimate relationship.

Be particularly careful with married men. For girls without daddies, men in unhappy marriages are absolutely not good candidates for friendship, let alone as candidates as surrogate father figures, because they are much more likely to be confused by your attention, particularly if you are young and attractive. Enter into male friendships being cognizant that men think differently than women and if you are leaning on the person as a surrogate father figure let him know that so he understands your goals in the relationship. Occasionally state that you view them like a father or a brother just to make sure he gets where you're coming from. Be aware of situations where your needs for male emotional intimacy might be interpreted by them as a desire for something more.

This chapter is more a word of caution against forming those friendships quickly and a reminder to be ever vigilant in making sure both parties understand the context of the relationship. Even if you are absolutely, utterly blunt, still be on guard as it seems that some men – not all – truly have a one-track mind.

15.

You Don't Need to Be Rescued by a Man

Does society promote the desire in all girls to be rescued by a man? Does this desire negatively affect the likelihood of their achieving a successful romantic relationship? Do girls without daddies have an even greater desire to be rescued by men than girls with daddies?

I'll warn you that I have some pretty strong beliefs on this topic, beliefs that I've paid dearly to develop. I am absolutely not a man hater. In fact, when I was in the workforce I believed that women perpetuated sex discrimination as much as men.

With that said, I believe our society promotes little girls' dreams of their knight in shining armor. Look at all the fairy tales girls grow up with: Cinderella, an abused young woman rescued by the all-powerful prince; Snow White, another abused young woman awakened by the prince's kiss; Sleeping Beauty, an abandoned young woman again awakened by the prince's kiss. The list goes on. We don't talk about a little boy's wedding day, yet little girls somehow end up dreaming of that one day in their life.

How does all this propaganda affect a girl's perspective on happiness for the rest of her life? It predisposes her to domestic roles typically subservient to men. Shake your head at me if you want, but it's true. If she doesn't find success as a wife, then isn't she more likely to be perceived as having a flaw.

Fortunately, this is less true today than it was in the past, but as long as the propaganda that we serve up to young girls promotes unrealistic fairy-tale rescues by men, there will be a gender road-block to the aspirations of women outside of romantic relation-ships. The irony is that these gender-defined boundaries will actu-ally pose a threat to their potential success in the fairy tale dream of romance because it establishes relationship imbalances from the outset that, as discussed, are difficult to overcome.

If I were to raise a daughter I would tell her from an early age that money would be aside for her college education plus a sepa-rate amount for her to use as she wished. If she wants a fancy wedding she can spend the money on that, or use it to make a down payment on a house, or travel to Europe after college, or any number of things. I would certainly hesitate to support any preconception that I'd write a blank check for some fairy-tale wed-ding. This is not pessimistic or suggestive that the marriage would fail. It just wouldn't support the dream of finding a man to whisk her away to the beginning of her fairy-tale life.

Let's take a look at how gender-defined roles are perpetuated in society by benevolent sexism. While this variety of sexism pres-ents a veneer of courtesy toward women, it really serves to confine women to their traditional domestic roles.[1] How does it manifest? The list is quite long.

Two personal examples can serve as illustrations of the point. They both came up in the same conversation, much to the angst of the poor man I was talking to. In New York for business meetings, my staff and I were being escorted by a sales agent. We stopped at a coffee shop in between meetings and began talking about a then-current topic: should the Augusta National Golf Club allow women to be members. Being the only woman there, I expressed the view that it would seem that allowing women would be advantageous because the conversations would be so much more interesting. In retrospect that was perhaps a small dig at men in general.

The sales agent began to explain that what I needed to understand was that the rules prohibiting women at Augusta were instituted back when, and I quote, "Women knew their place." I sensed all the men sitting around the table tense up, wondering how I'd respond. I quickly pondered how to make a point without being too blunt. Then I leaned toward him, laughed loudly and asked the poor salesman, "Can you believe you said that out loud?" Everyone around the table was visibly relieved and laughed a little too heartily.

The salesman's reaction was to try to assure me he had nothing but respect for women. He went on to prove this respect by telling me he had three female dependents on his tax return. That poor guy, he needed to stop while he was behind. At that point I took pity on him and said I understood the point he was trying to make.

How do his statements exhibit benevolent sexism? Without realizing how cemented in societal gender roles he was, the poor man showed his alleged respect for women with examples that confined them to traditional dependent roles – literally, as dependents on his tax return.

Here's another workplace example. At a former employer we were discussing candidates for a leadership program. A woman was selected but then it was volunteered – by a man – that she was pregnant and we shouldn't put pressure on her to decide between her career and her family at that sensitive time. All the men nodded in agreement.

I was shocked. "Nonsense," I said. I went on to explain that we should respect her ability to make those decisions for herself. She doesn't need us protecting her. We wouldn't do that for a man whose wife was pregnant! Quite the opposite would be true. We'd think he would welcome a promotion as it would help him provide better for his family.

Fortunately, I was heard and she was asked. She declined the program at that time but asked to be considered again. I was fine with her declining because at least she knew what we thought of her potential. And, more importantly, she was treated as competent to make decisions about how she balanced her personal and professional life rather than having men decide for her in order to protect her from that supposed heavy burden.

Now let's consider some simple examples of benevolent sexism that might not seem at all sexist. These courtesies include holding the door for women, letting women walk in front in a restaurant, walking on the outside of the sidewalk to protect a woman from potential danger from oncoming cars.

Before you object too vehemently, I freely admit I can see this from both sides. In fact, I've taught my son to hold doors open for women. My training efforts even included my stopping and standing at a door waiting for him to reach around and open it for me. I'm certainly not too weak to open the door. Have I taught my son to be subtly sexist? Perhaps. My hope is that I've only taught him a way to show respect while recognizing women are absolutely capable of opening their own doors. Nonetheless, the prevalence of these nice little gestures of kindness to women without clear delineation of their purpose can serve to perpetuate the continued subservience of women to men.

To understand how benevolent sexism might influence all girls, we need to look at the three different manifestations: paternalism, gender differentiation and heterosexuality.

- Paternalism has to do with a fatherly presence,
  protection and potentially dominance.

- Gender differentiation is important because it is the form of group identity that individuals develop first. It is also the strongest, as this identity establishes groups that have restrictions, and those restrictions often include endowing men with power (for many reasons, including physical size), which ultimately relegates women to more domestic roles.

- Heterosexuality is the one category where both parties have equal interests in a romantic relationship, thus serving to level the playing field. This equality puts the male in an unfamiliar vulnerable position. Not surprisingly, this vulnerability results in romantic relationships posing the greatest threat of violence toward women.[2]

Now let's look at how these types of benevolent sexism present greater challenges to girls without daddies.

- Paternalism. This one explains itself. What girl without a daddy wouldn't fall into the arms of a long-awaited protector, thus subjecting herself to a subservient and domestically dependent role?

- Gender differentiation. Given that this involves men's physicality, it will represent a potentially impassable quagmire to a girl without a daddy, as by definition she's not as knowledgeable about gender roles and is likely to be smaller and therefore more subject to physical intimidation.

- Heterosexuality. This one makes me sigh heavily, as it is the least comfortable role for men, making it the most dangerous for women and even more dangerous for girls without daddies who lack adequate tools to maintain a balance of power in the relationship. Given that a girl without a daddy is more likely to begin a romantic relationship with an empowerment deficit, it is easy to see how a vulnerable man can exude dominance to reclaim his comfort level, leaving room for the relationship to become abusive. This is where gender differentiation and heterosexuality play together.

Let's look at an early relationship I had right after getting away from my stepfather. I loved the guy so much. I thought I could never survive without him. Essentially, he was my rescuer. Through him I felt loved, worthy and safe. The question is: would I have felt as strongly toward him if I wasn't so needy? At this point I can safely say I would not.

Compounding this dilemma, my dependence gave him too much power. When things got out of balance, as a result of the natural disruptions that happen in any relationship, he began to use this power to control me. If he wanted something he'd use my insecurities to manipulate me. Even worse, when I began building my own independence through college activities he felt he was losing control. His attempts to get me back under his thumb intensified – this was my "marrying daddy" relationship. The liaison became emotionally abusive and physically threatening.

Let's look at this relationship in terms of benevolent sexism.

1. Paternalism – check. He was my rescuer.

2. Gender differentiation – check. As my success became evident through achievements in college, his need to drive me back into my gender-driven role intensified.

3. Heterosexuality – check. With gender differentiation becoming blurred for my knight in shining armor, his discomfort with vulnerability in the intimacy of our relationship increased, and so did the abusive nature of the relationship.

I hit the trifecta!

With almost no prep from a loving father figure, my learning about the realities of relationships coincided with my attempts at forming relationships. This left me at an immediate disadvantage with both selection and execution. Ultimately, I discovered there is no such thing as a knight in shining armor, and that realization was not even disappointing. I'd call it more of a reality adjustment.

After this psychological realignment, I could see the men I dated as normal fallible human beings, which was definitely to their advantage. I didn't expect my knight in shining armor to be omniscient. If something was important, I'd just let him know. This at least gave him a fighting chance if he was a little clueless. I didn't pout. I didn't hold grudges. I didn't over-personalize a guy's shortcomings. On the one hand, this was great because it removed a lot of unnecessary noise and drama out of relationships. On the other hand, my adjusted perspective narrowed the field of candidates considerably because, even though I had moved on from societal gender-defined roles, not all men found gender equality as appealing as I did.

That brings us back to a more global perspective. Is there hope for girls in the face of society's continuing predisposition to herd them into gender-defined roles subservient to men? Yes. There are wonderful men out there who want a balanced relationship. You just have to keep looking until you find that guy. Get used to the fact that it might take a lot of looking.

Ultimately, I abandoned all expectations of being rescued. Instead, I looked at a man and asked myself whether I would rescue him should he ever need it. I know a woman who was happily married to a wonderful, supportive man. After years of happy marriage, the man suffered an injury that left him a paraplegic. The woman ended up supporting and caring for her superhero. I'd be lying if I said it wasn't hard on her, but she took care of him regardless.

Would I be willing to take care of a potential romantic partner for the rest of his life, no matter what? Was I willing to be his knight in shining armor if needed? A marriage out of need has built-in obstacles, whereas a marriage out of true love "of" the other person at least has a fighting chance. If you find yourself thinking, "He loves me," ask yourself, "Do I really love him?"

So what do you do if you feel like you want to be rescued? Recognize that a relationship is doomed to get out of balance if it requires the woman to be rescued emotionally, or rescued domestically or doesn't allow for the emotional vulnerability of the man.

Readjust your perspective to put yourself on equal footing with men. Work patiently on yourself until you can exist on that equal footing. Finally, patiently look for the right man. Ultimately, a healthy relationship is all about balance.

16.

Are You Attractive?

Are you attractive? What's interesting about this question is how we interpret it. Is your first thought that the question is about outward appearance? Or do you think about your whole self? Those that think about outward beauty are more focused on self-image, whereas those whose first thought goes to the overall person are leaning more toward self-esteem.

Deepak Chopra says, "There is a difference between self-esteem and self-image. The reason people have all this plastic surgery is because they have actually forgotten themselves and are identifying themselves with their self-image. The real Self within you is beneath no one. It's immune to criticism and it's fearless. Do not confuse your image with your Self – your self-image is what other people think of you, and your Self (esteem) is what you think of you."[1].

Basically self-esteem is the value you see yourself having in the world. 'Am I a worthwhile human being?'[2].

In my view, your self-esteem drives how the world sees you. It drives your self-image. In fact, it drives how you interpret and answer the question, "Are you attractive?"

Society places substantial emphasis on physical appearance, particularly for girls. We are constantly bombarded with marketing messages showing us the standard to which we should aspire.

Anyone with weak self-esteem can easily become obsessed with measuring up to these external standards of self-image.

This dilemma is not unique to girls either with or without daddies. We've addressed how girls without daddies are lacking in self-esteem. "A blog that was posted in website 'Love-Life Learning Center' created by Dr. Tom Jordan and his wife, whose professions are in the field of psychology, states that fathers need to nurture their daughters in order for them to have a secure sense of themselves as individuals and as desirable women."[3]

This suggests that girls without daddies sadly lack the influence of their fathers in developing a secure sense of themselves, leaving them at a disadvantage in how they view their attractiveness.

My experience is a case in point. My sister is 16 months older than me. When I was little, I always viewed her as absolutely beautiful and still do. We don't look much alike and in high school people were always shocked to find out we were sisters.

When she was about 15 years old, my mom signed her up for modeling lessons. Of course, this reinforced my impression that my sister was beautiful and I was okay-looking, as my mother never asked whether I was interested in modeling lessons.

My sister learned how to put on make-up, dress up and all those girly things. I, on the other hand, am still not entirely convinced I do a decent job putting on my makeup. As a result, I went through the remainder of my childhood and part of my adult life with the impression that my sister was beautiful and I was something less than that.

Many years later, I mentioned to my mother the conclusion I had drawn about her giving my sister modeling lessons. My mom almost fell off her chair. Looking at me aghast, she uttered, "Didn't you ever notice how your sister walked?" I did recall that my sister used to have a tendency to throw her feet out to each side when she walked. My mother then went on to tell me that the modeling lessons were her solution for helping my sister learn to walk in a more feminine manner.

I started laughing but my mother felt awful. In my case, I took something completely irrelevant and drew a less than positive conclusion, which stayed with me for years. That misinterpretation affected my self-image. How did I shore up this deficit?

Let's first consider what makes a woman truly attractive? Consider the synonyms for the word "attract" from the online dictionary at merriam-webster.com: "allure, charm, captivate, fascinate, enchant... to draw another by exerting a powerful influence."

With this definition in mind, I have observed many women to assess how their behavior and presentation affected my view of their attractiveness. I learned quickly that a physically beautiful person could quickly become quite ugly if their personality was offensive. And I learned that someone that I might have originally assessed as plain can be sparklingly attractive because of their personality.

Through observation, I learned that a big smile and eye contact is all you really need to captivate someone's attention. When a person thinks they are a worthwhile human being, it shows in how they present and carry themselves, and ultimately they attract people and attention. How you view yourself affects how other people view you. Your self-esteem affects your self-image.

Here's an example of how attractiveness can be demonstrated in a way that has nothing to do with physical beauty. In the book, *Love Must Be Tough* by James C. Dobson, the author discusses his dating relationship with his future wife. They had separated for a bit early in their dating and her confidence about the breakup literally drew him back in. She didn't grovel or beg or ask what she'd done wrong when he wanted a break. She simply said OK and appeared to move on confidently with her life, leaving him to wonder if he'd just thrown back the best fish he could catch.

I've taken liberties with my recall of this example but the point is that self-confidence is a big hook if you want to catch a great fish. Lack of self-confidence is also a great way to go fishing without bait. Fishing without bait is likely to be unproductive and even worse might yield some pretty desperate fish on the line. And, as already pointed out, once girls without daddies are in a relationship they can have a hard time getting out. You could get stuck with a fish you never wanted to catch.

Another example is Oprah Winfrey. I consider her a non-traditional beauty. If you really examine her facial features she might not measure up to the commercialized standards of attractiveness. Yet, she is stunning. Why? She is attractive both because of how she presents herself physically and because she exudes a belief that she is a worthwhile human being. Her self-esteem transforms her into a non-traditional beauty. She presents herself as attractive and therefore we see her as such.

The bottom line is that you can be perceived as attractive if you perceive yourself as attractive. Your physical appearance is just the way you were made. If you are physically beautiful, great! Life is likely going to be a tad easier for you. In some cases, it can be too easy. I once dated a young man who told me he preferred dating women who were ugly ducklings when they were young. He found they were much more interesting compared to women who had beauty to open doors easily. If you don't perceive yourself to be physically beautiful, change your perspective and view yourself as a former ugly duckling now transforming into a beautiful swan, powered by the experience of all the hard work it took to get those doors to open.

How does a girl without a daddy develop a secure sense of self that lets her believe – and therefore be – attractive? The following excerpt, by Asoka Selvarajah PhD on the selfgrowth.com website, was so spot-on in terms of how I addressed the deficit in my "self" that I'm including it in its entirety:

> *The key is NOT to work upon self-image. This is what many people try to do. However, working on self-esteem is the heart of creating radical change. When you work from the inside out, how you feel about yourself in comparison with externals must eventually improve as well.*

> *The key to improving your self-esteem is to take conscious control of your self-talk. Negative self-talk is the prime cause for creating and maintaining negative self-esteem. The things you say to yourself in your mind, as well as the meaning you attribute to events in your life, combine to create the reality you end up living. Most people's self-talk is roughly 95% negative. They see the worst in themselves and in everything that happens. Putting a stop to such self-destructive thinking is vital. It is our thoughts and expectations that shape and produce what we become. The quality of our lives is a direct result of them.*

> *One excellent way to combat and overcome negative self-talk is through using positive affirmations. The principle behind them is that the brain cannot entertain two contradictory notions at the same time. Eventually one of the two contradictory notions must win out and cause the other to collapse completely. The belief that finally wins out is the one that you invest with the most emotional energy and constancy of thought.*

> *Affirmations such as:*

> *"I like myself."*

"I am a positive person and I create a positive life."

"I am a wonderful person of immense value who deserves to be loved."

These and others like them will do absolute wonders. Note how all good affirmations are framed in the positive. Never frame an affirmation in the negative, e.g. "I am NOT a negative person." The subconscious literally cannot see the word "not" and will therefore interpret and act upon the affirmation as if you said "I AM a negative person.[4]

In addition to affirmations, practice throwing those shoulders back and holding the position for as long as you can. Do it over and over until it becomes a new habit. Practice this with your smile, too. Smile like you have the whole world at your feet. Again, do this for as long as you can each time and then do it over and over until it becomes a new habit.

Focus your energy on making this world a beautiful place and in the end you will smile with your whole heart and be beautiful as well.

17.

Are You an Optimist or a Pessimist?

One of my favorite mottos is: Truth Prevails. Maybe it's what some people call Karma. Maybe I'm just an optimist. The real question is whether one's expectations of how things will turn out actually affects the real-life outcome. [1] I don't mean through mental frequencies, as described in *The Secret* by Rhonda Byrne,[2] but rather does optimism directly result in better outcomes when compared to pessimism? And, do girls with and without daddies have different tendencies in the optimistic/pessimistic balance? If they lean toward pessimism, can they tilt this tendency the other way?

I'm not suggesting that a Polly Anna transformation is the ultimate goal. Pessimism has its advantages. It can help identify potential issues in advance and enable a person to avoid problems altogether. I spent a lot of my career working in risk management. You can't manage risk without identifying it first. This involves being able to see negative outcomes. As there are sunny days and rainy days, so also must there be optimism and pessimism. Yet life under the constant cover of dark clouds is certainly not desirable and, in my view, neither is a dominantly pessimistic perspective.

Let's begin with the definition of optimism from dictionary.com:

- A disposition or tendency to look on the more favorable side of events or conditions and to expect the most favorable outcome

- The belief that good ultimately predominates over evil in the world

- The belief that goodness pervades reality

- The doctrine that the existing world is the best of all possible worlds.

Does optimism actually change outcomes? "Research has shown that optimism is correlated with many positive life outcomes including increased life expectancy, general health, better mental health, increased success in sports and work, greater recovery rates from heart operations and better coping strategies when faced with adversity."[3]

When you look at the list of benefits, do you see a correlation between cause and effect? For example, if I think I will succeed at work I'm more likely to work hard, apply for promotions and therefore be successful. If I think I will live a long life I'm more likely to take care of my body and as a result I live a longer life.

Conversely, a pessimist believes she won't be successful and therefore never tries, creating a similar but opposite self-fulling prophecy. Optimism and pessimism in these cases lead directly to definitive outcomes. This, of course, does not eliminate the rather more nebulous outcomes from optimism (and pessimism,) such as better (or worse) mental health, etc.

Most people are optimistic. In a gender-based case study done by Shruti Singh and Sunita Mishra, the following results were noted: "Males and females respondents were predominantly optimistic and very optimistic, respectively. Fortunately, very few of them reported pessimistic and very pessimistic."[4]

As for girls with and without daddies, a study by Suman Lata and Surender Kumar Sharma on the influence of parental encouragement on optimistic versus pessimistic attitudes of adolescents is revealing:

"Parental encouragement is of great importance in developing psychological as well as academic behaviour of the child. Parental encouragement has great impact on optimistic and pessimistic attitude of adolescents. But the present study shows that it is not only parental encouragement that affects the optimistic and pessimistic attitude of students, there may be various other factors that play a more important role in comparison to parental encouragement in developing optimistic and pessimistic attitudes, such as social factors, economic factors."[5]

From this study's conclusion, it appears fatherless children in general could easily tend toward pessimism, given the obvious lack of at least one parent's encouragement. Add to that the influence from other important social and economic factors specific to girls without daddies – higher poverty rates, higher adolescent pregnancy rates, higher suicide rates, higher rates of behavioral problems, and lower educational achievement[6] – and it's easy to see that girls without daddies can easily have a greater disposition toward pessimism.

While some research indicates optimism can be learned, there is some opposition to that conclusion. It is generally agreed that optimism is a cognitive skill, which is an ability used to learn.

Consider the following: "Research is encouraging that, whilst optimism may be dispositional, it can indeed be learned. It has less inherited aspects than some of the other dispositional traits and as such is responsive to interventions. Segerstrom asserts her thesis in her book, *Breaking Murphy's Law*: 'The thesis of this book is that optimists are happy and healthy not because of who they are but because of how they act.' (p. 167). Optimism is more what we do than what we are, and thereby can be learned."[7]

That's good news for girls without daddies, if in fact they have tended toward the pessimistic end of the scale. You can work toward being optimistic.

In my own case I might be something of an outlier as an optimistic girl without a daddy. You can probably see how tempting it might be to live in the shadow of the things that were "done to me," to add up the wrongs and bemoan them. Why, then, am I an optimist? It's those surrounding circumstances, which in my case was my mother.

While I might not have gotten a great toolbox from my father, she provided me with some special training that made a huge difference in how I looked at things. That outlook adjustment prevented me from tending to expect negative outcomes.

My mother had a very black-and-white view of right and wrong, which became instilled in me. If I found a dime in a store, I was required to offer it to an employee because it did not belong to me and its owner might notice it missing. Fortunately, my mother was adaptive in her training. One day, I found a quarter in a variety store and followed the usual instructions. When I offered it to a young female employee, she giggled, thanked me and said she'd just keep it. She slipped the quarter in her pocket and walked away.

I can still remember the look on my mother's face when I turned around. She walked up to me and said, "From now on you can just keep any change you find." With that, I learned the practicalities of justice. She had taught me right from wrong, but she also taught me to apply reason to situations. This is different from learning how to rationalize wrongdoing. My mother's training simply differentiated between an idealistic truth and a practical truth.

Let's contrast this found quarter situation to something that had what seemed at the time to be dramatic consequences. At around seven years old, I had a friend who was not such a good influence –you might even wonder who the bad influence in this story actually was.

While I don't remember initiating the endeavor, I take responsibility for its creativity and its execution. The short version is that we created fake quarters out of these little cardboard cutouts we found in some packaging. We took them to the store and stood at the little candy machines for a long time, deciding whether or not to proceed with the plan. My friend, the not-so-good influence, either knew better or was too afraid and refused to use her fake quarters.

However, I couldn't imagine going to all that effort and then not following through. I used my fake quarter and out of the machine dropped a little round plastic ball that contained two stunning totally fake diamond rings. My friend then threatened me that if I did not give her one of the diamond rings, she would tell. I refused, thinking her ridiculous. How was taking one of my rings any different from her using her own fake quarter? She would be equally guilty.

Apparently, logic was irrelevant. She immediately went through the store in search of my mother, quickly found her and snitched on me. Within five minutes my mother had marched me into the intimidating manager's office of this large retail store. I had to confess my crime, give him both the fake diamond rings, all my fake quarters and, worst of all, I had to give him the real quarter my mother had given me to use in the machine.

And the finale? My sister and I were forbidden from ever using those machines for the rest of our lives – we got two life sentences! It's important to note that my sister was completely unaware of my heinous crime until I was turned in by my co-conspirator. Yet she was punished right along with me. I learned that my actions could hurt innocent people around me.

From these types of experiences, my mother instilled in me an understanding that when people cheat they hurt others. She showed me that the only way to lose my integrity was to give it away through misdeeds. It also became apparent that I would eventually be caught, so any victory would be short-lived, if one could call successful theft a victory. Basically, my mother taught me about consequences for my actions.

There is also the slight possibility that she was sick and tired of giving us money for those stupid machines and saw this as an outstanding opportunity to never have to do that again.

Experiences on cause and effect, as taught by my mother, led to my beginning to notice how many times wrongs are righted. Sometimes I've been frightened by how quickly others' wrongs were brought to light and consequences ensued. If they get their comeuppance, does that mean I will always get mine? After all, I know I'm not perfect and I don't want to be hunted down for all my wrongs. This type of thought process has enabled me to forgive many inadvertent wrongs whose consequences affected me.

Other examples of wrongs being righted came to my attention as an auditor. People who stole money from their employers were inevitably caught and held accountable. Later in my career I saw fellow co-workers attempt to sabotage other co-workers and ultimately the saboteur would lose their job because of their malicious efforts.

Another more grotesque experience was my stepfather forcing me to eat the fat on my pork chop, a huge amount of fat that should have been cut off before cooking, something to reflect on as his health declined before his ultimate death from heart disease.

Would I have noticed these corrections if I had not been look-ing? My belief that the truth prevails drove me to make these obser-vations and bolstered my optimism. It taught me that regardless of what other people do, I should do the right thing because they weren't getting away with anything and neither would I. It kept me from giving up. It kept me from feeling victimized because, no matter what, eventually things would even out.

Does it seem a bit backwards that believing other people can't get away with crap made me optimistic? See point 2 in the defini-tion of happiness noted above: "The belief that good ultimately predominates over evil in the world."

If you don't believe that the truth, and therefore justice, will prevail, is it because you've never seen it? Have you never seen it because you never looked for it? I understand this might be laugh-able to a person who has been victimized. If I hadn't been put through honesty boot camp by my mother, I believe I could have lived through all the same experiences and never have noticed the truth prevailing because, without believing it possible, why would I even bother to look?

Let's consider happiness in general. Is happiness genetically determined or is it within our influence? Studies indicate that the answer is about half-genetic and half by choice or focus.[8]

What I take from this is if you don't feel like smiling, smile any-way. When the muscles in your face form a smile, this send signals to your body that you are happy.[9]

Do this over and over and build a new perspective on life with the 50 percent of your happiness you have control of. Even if your genetics give you a disadvantage, if there is at least one happy genetic percentage point then you can win at 51 percent happi-ness by contributing the half you have control over.

Consider this conclusion to the study on happiness: "We need to stop chasing happiness and start seeking brief moments of fun and meaningfulness. Savoring experiences, practicing gratitude, and cultivating mindfulness all help to increase enjoyment and pleasure in what we do and, hence, increase levels of happiness in our day-to-day enjoyment of life. When we can do this particularly well, we have the opportunity to influence not only our own well-being but also the well-being of our family, friends and wider community."[10]

What I would like you to take away from this chapter is a belief that if you look for good, you will find it. If you look for bad, you will find it. Try to develop a habit of looking for the good. Hold out hope that you can succeed even though you might not have been given an adequate toolbox to deal with the potholes in life. Hold out hope that when someone does you harm, that their path is their own and the consequences will be their own.

As it says in the good book, "Do unto others as you would have them do to you." (Luke 6:31) Live by this motto and you will become known for your integrity and that, in and of itself, will become your reward, as it will open doors for you that you might not even be able to imagine.

The bottom line is that instead of defaulting to a mentality that the world is against you, develop a mentality of optimism that good things will come your way. The old golf adage of "never up, never in" comes to mind. It you don't putt hard enough to reach the hole, your ball can never drop in it. If you don't have hope, you won't try. If you don't try, it won't happen. Always keep believing and trying, no matter how much you want to give up on the world.

18.

When Daddy Returns

How many television shows have you seen where the prodigal father turns up in his child's adult life wanting a reconciliation? We see them frequently. Typically, in the movies anyway, the wayward father discovers he's thrown out the important things in life and now wants to make amends. Essentially, he wants his cake and he plans to eat it, too. This might be one topic on which I don't have much optimism.

Society seems to place great value in forgiveness of wayward parents, even to the point of expecting the abandoned child to care for errant parents in their declining years. There is a sense that to heal one should forgive. In addition, there is great societal pressure on adult children to make efforts at these reconciliations even when the prodigal parent was abusive.[1]

My view is if you get something out of it, go for it. Otherwise, you are under no obligation. Be realistic about your expectations for an apology as it's doubtful your prodigal father can fully comprehend how his absence affected you. If he does get the picture, and his understanding is not a new revelation, it makes his absence all the more egregious.

Still, I tried. In my twenties I used to bike a lot. One day I rode out to my grandfather's just to say hi. During our conversation, my grandfather told me my father needed me because his wife was dying – both my father and his wife were in their mid-fifties.

It was a convoluted conversation for a couple of reasons. One, my grandfather had a stroke a couple of years earlier and speaking was frustratingly difficult for him. When he finally articulated his concern, he would slam his hand on the table simultaneously. Two, I didn't have the heart to tell him that I really didn't give a damn, as I rarely saw my father and he was anything but the model parent. If my grandfather hadn't figured it out on his own, hearing it from me was unlikely to penetrate the happy bubble he was living in anyway. I opted for a sympathetic smile and said I understood.

A few months later I got a call from my father. He told me my grandfather was in the hospital and the situation was critical. When I arrived at the hospital, my father was in the waiting room and said that my grandfather would die soon.

Although my grandfather had a perfectly treatable condition, he had asked for no extraordinary measures, which in this case involved penicillin for pneumonia. He had lived all the life he wanted to at that point. His wife had been dead for some time. I could see it in his eyes when I had visited him that couple of months earlier. After my grandfather died, my father asked me to meet him at grandfather's place to pick out any things I might want. I went.

The other invitee was my father's wife. She was terribly skinny. Her head was wrapped to hide the consequences of chemotherapy. Yet, there she was picking her treasures out of my grandfather's belongings. She had already laid claim to the only item I had any interest in. It was of little consequence to me, but my father whispered I'd get it soon enough as she wouldn't be around very long.

These details are relevant as these were the only real interactions I'd had with my father for years. Not long after, he called and asked me to dinner. This, too, was odd but I accepted the invitation. At that dinner, my father told me that he needed me because his wife was dying and he couldn't go through it alone. Those words ran through my head repeatedly after that dinner. "I can't go through this alone."

Soon after I had to head out of town on a work assignment. I got into the hotel room late but hardly slept. Those words, "I can't go through this alone," ran through my head. On the one hand, there was my daddy with his arms out to me. On the other hand, what right did that bastard have leaning on me for anything? It became one of those, "I can't not do it" situations. I decided I'd be there for him so he "wasn't alone."

Fortunately, it was only one month later that his wife died. I say fortunately only because my investment in this process was fairly short-lived, as was the alleged reconciliation my father wanted with me. Shortly after his wife's death he began dating a woman and lost all interest in me. That woman was his ex-wife, my mother, which I'm sure you can imagine brought its own load of crap with it.

As it turns out, my father was sick, too. A few months later my mom got a call from a hospital in a nearby city. My dad had a seizure on a layover for a business trip to Taiwan. We drove to the hospital, where the doctor informed us that if he woke up he would likely not be able to speak and in any case he would die in six to nine months as there was nothing that could be done for the type of cancer he had.

He died seven months later. His death put an end to any further attempt by him at building a relationship with me. Did that bother me? No, it wouldn't have mattered. He'd used up his last chance anyway. I know I might sound bitter but I'm really not. I gave it a shot. I cried. I learned that his stripes hadn't changed.

For some girls without daddies, their wayward fathers will someday get old and may gain some perspective on what is important in life and attempt a reconciliation. Other fathers may simply want someone to come and change their diapers and feed them in their old-age while offering nothing in return. Should these fathers be afforded the gift of your love or support even though they failed to be there for you when you were in the greatest need? It's up to you. In my opinion, you owe them nothing.

If I were to go through my thought process on this decision now, I'd evaluate it just like any new relationship. And I'd make sure I could get out of it, just like any other new relationship. That's probably the finance person in me balancing the scales. But life, and therefore my time, is precious. I don't want to waste my energy in the bottomless pit of a relationship, even if it is with the father whose love I had so longed for as a little girl.

Give what you want but be careful. Are you strong enough to develop a healthy relationship with a person to whom you might be too vulnerable? Will you be able to walk away if it becomes destructive to you? Are you subjecting others in your life, such as your children, to a high-risk relationship? There are some relationships, even close family relationships, that are simply too unhealthy for your personal growth and long-term happiness.

All that being said, if you have the self-confidence to move forward, knowing the potential pitfalls, then the effort might be worth the learning experience. There is always the possibility of some healing and possibly a chance of a long-term healthy relationship. Consider professional counseling, individually and possibly jointly with your father.

If you decide not to give your wayward father another chance, counseling should still be considered as you might be surprised by how emotionally vulnerable you felt when the phone rang and daddy said he loves you after all.

19.

Faith as a Tool

You may read the title of this chapter and think, "Oh brother, here we go." Many believe that religion is a coping mechanism. It's something that helps us accept uncertainty, accept mortality and believe that everything happens for a reason. I can't say that's not partly true. If you are one of those people, feel free to skip this chapter, but you might give it a try as my journey on this road might at least amuse you.

My rocky introduction to religion began in a small group of six-year-olds as we were driven home from Sunday school by our Sunday school teacher. I accepted Christ in her car because, according to her, my alternative was to burn in the fires of hell. The choice seemed like a no-brainer. My introduction to God was to either love him or be tortured by him for eternity. These options are not exactly what I would expect from a loving god. This conclusion is why I believe the god of fiery hell to be the version of God created by man to control his fellow man.

Fast-forward a few years. When I was nine, my mother got engaged to a Catholic man, my future stepfather. He wanted to remain Catholic, so he needed an annulment from his former wife and mother of his four children. Nothing says a marriage never existed like four children!

To accomplish this annulment – and facilitate our own conversion – my sister and I had to learn what was involved in being a Catholic, which meant lessons from nuns. As the obedient pleaser, I dutifully memorized the assigned prayers and completed all the required reading until this entire process came to an abrupt end. I can thank my non-compliant sister for my lack of bended knee every Sunday since.

It all ended during a lesson when my sister, who questioned everything, disagreed with the nun. I don't recall the exact biblical dispute, but I remember the skirt of the nun's habit flying across my face as she pulled me in one hand and my sister in the other across the courtyard to where the priest was meeting with my mother and soon-to-be stepfather.

When we entered the room, the nun used her grasp on our little hands to yank us forward and announce we were never to be brought back. Then she abruptly left us there. My career as a Catholic had ended before it began. Needless to say, there was no annulment and my stepfather was ex-communicated. This experience gave me my permission slip to continue seeing organized religion as nonsensical.

Even though my attitude to organized religion is skeptical, it is not a blanket suspicion. In my adult years, I began breeding and showing miniature horses. Before I go on to my point, for the sake of my fellow breeders I feel compelled to say these horses are not just cute – they are beautiful representations of what an Arabian horse looks like in miniature form.

Back to my point, my miniature horse adventures include using a professional trainer and often befriending other clients who also use that trainer. In one case, to my surprise my fellow clients included nuns. At first when I saw them walking down the aisle with their habits blowing behind them, I diverted my path to avoid an encounter. This approach would be a short-lived escape, as at times we all spent days or even weeks at horse shows.

Once I dismissed my negative predisposition toward the nuns, I found they were nothing like my single encounter with the nun that rejected my sister and me. In fact, they are the most kind, loving, and accepting people I have encountered in my life. I now look forward to seeing them, and even miss them during long stretches between shows.

I don't presume to fully comprehend their belief system, but from my many conversations with them it seems very much like mine – a simple faith filled with love and not complicated with dogma. My point is that one should not cast a wide net over a group because of a single negative experience with an alleged representative of that group. If I had continued on my judgmental path toward organized religion I would have missed an opportunity to know these amazingly loving people with whom I had some of my most cherished conversations about faith and religion.

Like many others, I've had other unpleasant experiences with organized religion. The details aren't relevant but the conclusion is. Just like people outside the church, people inside the church are not perfect. Problems arise when the folks in the church tend to forget this. I actually heard a woman in the church once refer to the "sinners outside." This attitude is off-putting, to say the least.

With those experiences in mind, why do I believe in God? There were some key moments when I felt like God was really there for me. I had a young marriage. The relationship started when I was sixteen and was an escape from the many issues with my stepfather as well as a substitute for the things I was seeking as a girl without a daddy.

The point is that I ended the marriage. Subsequently, the thought haunted me that, since it was I that had ended the marriage, I was somehow not free to remarry. Go figure. Of course, now I would like to slap my younger self in the face. Nonetheless, I had some guilt.

As I struggled with this for several years, a strong sense emerged that I would come across my ex-husband at a road run I was about to go on. This premonition was completely unfounded as I hadn't seen him for years and when we were married he had criticized my running as a ridiculous activity that would only serve to wear down my body.

At the end of this race, standing in the crowd of about 5,000 runners, I looked to my left and sure enough there he was, just as I had intuited. He had become a runner, which I later learned was in the hopes of encountering me again. To my horror he wanted to discuss a reconciliation and, of course, my dogmatic religious guilt compelled me to pursue this ludicrous idea.

We agreed on a day to meet to discuss this potential reconciliation. In the interim I went out of town on a business trip. At night I rubbed my elbows raw on the cheap hotel sheets as I tossed and turned, hounded by my doctrinaire religious deliberation. Finally, I felt obligated to give reconciliation a try – obviously, not the same decision I would make today.

When we met again, my ex was quite uncomfortable. He had some news and he was sure it would not sit well with me. His news? He had a girlfriend, who he currently lived with, and she was pregnant. I almost laughed out loud. In fact, I might have laughed out loud.

For the entire time I had been grappling with this absurd religious dilemma the die had already been cast. I had somehow been protected, as a reconciliation was never really possible. Of course, I told him that I could not imagine a God that would want a woman to reconcile with her former spouse at the expense of his current girlfriend and now future child.

My ex-spouse went on to have three daughters with his girl-friend, whereas I was set free. I had been trapped by religious dogma but God had been watching out for me the entire time. He never intended a reconciliation but He could see my heart's desire was to do what I thought was the right thing. He simply showed me the dogma of my thinking and freed me from it. Now, that's a God I can get behind, one who helps me past the unfathomable dogma promulgated by the people in His own church!

Further clarity on what I should expect from a loving God came the day my son was born. His dad and I created this little human being. Now as a man I see his strengths and weaknesses and I love them both. I see them as an integral part of who he is. To the extent that he is less than perfect, I love him no less. I hope the best for him. I want happiness for him. I would do anything for him.

Trust me, I am not God-like. I imagine how much more perfect the love of an all-knowing, all-powerful God would be. Would a true God need me to say certain words or cower in fear? Would He need me to be perfect and would he look away from me when I failed? The only way that is possible is if He is less loving than I am, and that's not a God that sounds very godlike. If this God created me, then He knows my strengths and weaknesses and thoughts. He also knows the circumstances around my life, whether that be rich or poor, fathered or fatherless.

How can a God that created me and put me in my circumstances have anything but love and compassion and understanding? My guess is He's rooting for me to simply overcome the obstacles in my path and grow as I move forward. Despite watching mistake after mistake, he's still in the stands cheering me on. This is the

God I love. If love holds no record of wrongs, then why would God? Would he call us to a standard that he himself doesn't feel the need to follow?

I don't care what mistakes you have made. I don't care how many people you have hurt. Whatever you have done, the God I love will accept you back willingly at any moment because His love for you is unimaginably beyond any human's love for their own child.

As food for thought on this topic, let me share excerpts from an article by David C. Pack, online at realtruth.org, titled "The Existence of God – Logically Proven!" While some of the proof seems to require a predisposition toward a belief in God, two of the points require the least inclination and the third you might simply find amusing:

- "The First Law of Thermodynamics is stated as follows: matter and energy can be neither created nor destroyed. The proof to this point was that if matter and energy cannot be created or destroyed, and radioactive elements give off radiation at a set pace over time and they transform into other less radioactive elements, how could radiation have always existed? This represents absolute proof that matter came into existence or, in other words, matter has not always existed!"

- "The Second Law of Thermodynamics is best summarized by saying that everything moves toward disorder – or a condition known as entropy... Like a top or a yo-yo, the universe must have been 'wound up.' Since the universe is constantly winding down, the second law of

thermodynamics looms before us in the form
of a great question: who wound it up? The only
plausible answer is God!"

- "As for the big bang theory: "Dr. B.G. Ranganathan
  said, '...the probability of life originating from
  accident is comparable to the unabridged
  dictionary resulting from an explosion in a printing
  shop' (Origins?)."[1]

These excerpts are not intended to convince you of the existence of God. Rather, as is the case with my examples, it seems that a disposition toward that belief can be supported by how we look at things. You are free to believe whatever you believe because forced believing is not believing at all.

Now my faith is as simple as that of a child's. With Him I've long ago put away any pretenses. He knows my heart. There's no point hiding my emotions or true desires. When I pray, it is to the loving supportive father that I never had in human form. I tell Him my deepest fears and my true desires. I talk about what I am going through and express myself fully and completely. At times, I simply feel better after having expressed myself.

Many times, I've found wisdom, clarity of thought, and direction that had previously eluded me. I don't understand everything about this supernatural being I call God, but I believe He is watching out for me in big and little ways and cares deeply for me.

Perhaps I owe more than I realize to the Sunday School teacher that scared the crap out of me as a child. It would have been impossible to survive my youth without some form of faith system.

If you've had a bad experience with people in the church and turned away from the pursuit of God because of it, remember they are fallible people too. They are not the God you seek. You don't have to give them another chance but that doesn't mean you can't give God another try.

If you're a girl without a daddy and also have no faith system, hopefully you have some kind of support system that can help you through whatever struggles life has in store for you.

Obviously, you cannot just wish yourself a faith system. No one can convince you there is a god that loves you. And I'm certainly not attempting to convince you there is, because that's an empty pursuit. Instead, I can only speak from my experiences and if they reach out to you, then great. If they do not, hopefully you keep searching for something that can give you hope and strength.

If you are interested in any reading on this topic, here are my favorite books: *Mere Christianity* by C.S. Lewis; *Christian Agnostic* by Leslie D. Weatherhead; *Last Days Madness: Obsession of the Modern Church* by Gary DeMar. Not being a huge fan of organized religion, I caution you that these books may present non-traditional perspectives on Christianity and organized religion.

In any case, I can only say that my faith was a fundamental part of helping me cope and survive. My hope for you is that, if you do not have a faith system, you open your heart to the idea of it. Just as the biological aspects of our lives are ordered by the table of the elements, I believe the spiritual connectivity among us all is similarly ordered by the All-Loving and All-Accepting.

20.

Divorce is Ugly

There is no question that divorce can be ugly, and certainly our society gives divorced parents permission to be uncooperative and spiteful. When two people who at one point loved each other enough to commit to a life-long relationship decide to turn on one another, the people who pay the most are their daughters. A case study done on the Effects of Parental Divorce on Marital Commitment and Confidence found that, "Experiencing a parental divorce appears to have a stronger impact on women's than men's desires and beliefs about the future of their own marriages."[1]

If you are a mother going through a divorce, how can you limit the chances that your divorce will have lasting negative effects on your daughter? If you are a woman whose parents divorced, what happened in that post-divorce era that may have negatively affected your behaviors today?

Several key factors are consistently identified as critical for limiting long-term negative consequences for children of divorce:

- Minimizing parental conflict

- Maintaining optimal parenting

- Maintaining economic stability

- Maintaining support from outside the family

- Minimizing risks from remarriage[2]

Before we look further into each category, it's helpful to recognize that many of these risk factors are not independent of each other. For example, parental conflict often leads to suboptimal parenting because the parents are consumed with fighting, are anxious and short-tempered and emotionally unavailable to their children. A decline in economic circumstances can lead to movement to more affordable housing, taking the children from the stability of nearby family, and friends.

Minimizing parental conflict is an obvious way to reduce stress for children after a divorce. This is easier said than done for parents in the immediate post-divorce period of pain and insecurity. The conflict can be exacerbated if a parent looks to their child for support, as this only stresses the child even more. I'm tempted to rant on this topic but instead here are a few personal examples of how both parental conflict and parental support affected me as a child of divorce.

This is the story of how I quit talking. When my parents divorced, I initially didn't think much about the impact on them. Being a child, I thought more about me. I got to live in an apartment with lots of kids around. We had a swimming pool. My ready acceptance of my parent's decision to divorce might have been because they fought openly before their separation. Studies show that children tend to adjust to divorce better when the conflict is high prior to the divorce, as opposed to a surprise divorce in cases where parents sought to protect children and hid pre-divorce conflict.[3]

Over time I became aware of the continuing discord between my parents. The key turning point for me was at one of my dad's work Christmas parties, where he introduced the woman he had been dating. He referred to her as his wife. I asked him about this, to which he replied that he had "kind of" gotten married.

Returning home, I casually told my mother that Daddy had "kind of" got married. She rather loudly retorted that you cannot kind of get married. She went on to say that it was like being kind of pregnant. You are either pregnant or you're not. You are either married or you're not. Her rant went on for a while, but it was long enough.

Looking back now, I can see that hearing that news was terribly painful for her. I had no grasp of the magnitude of what I was revealing. In fact, that is probably the only time I remember her exploding like that. Needless to say, I realized something was going on that I didn't understand. As a result, in order to avoid causing either of my parents any pain that I couldn't anticipate, I resolved to be very careful from then on about what I would say to either of them.

Unfortunately, my new protocol to protect my parents had real-life repercussions. I became accustomed to dealing with things myself. After a few years I really didn't talk about anything of significance with anyone. I'd just deal with problems as best I could.

This survival skill backfired in my teenage years. Instead of seeking counsel from my mother on important issues, such as drugs and guys, I just did my best to make my way through unaided. Let me summarize by saying I would have been well-served by a little adult guidance. Only as an adult could I look back and wonder why I never talked to anyone about what was going on in my life. Then I began to realize the devastation that my parent's divorce had on my openness in my youth.

Now for a mostly good example. I didn't get any gifts from my father on my ninth birthday. A few days later my mom gave me three gifts, all wrapped up, which she said my father had dropped off for me. It was amazing. They were all things I'd eyed in the store. I couldn't believe my father knew what I wanted. One gift was a toy robotic dog. The leash was a wire and I could hold the control at the end of the wire and make the dog walk and bark. I took this dog all around the apartment buildings bragging to my friends about how my father had given this to me for my birthday. I was so happy and proud.

Flash forward to my 27th year, when my dad wanted to reconcile with me. As we were chatting he mentioned the one year he forgot my birthday. I was puzzled for about ten seconds. Then it dawned on me. My dad didn't give me those gifts. My mother went out and bought them, wrapped them and gave them to me, just to protect me from knowing that my dad had forgotten about me.

Can you imagine the love involved on her part in doing that? Can you imagine her seeing me brag about my dad and how much he loved me and how well he knew what I wanted, all the while knowing none of that was true? She never said a word. I thanked her for that wonderful gift of love eighteen years too late. Amusingly, after the year of the dog, birthday presents from my father consisted of a $50 check in the mail each year because he said he didn't know what I'd want.

A second positive example is how my son's father and I dealt with our divorce. Being a child of divorce, I worried about how divorce would affect our son. As a result, one of my terms in the divorce agreement was that we go to dinner as a family regularly and socialize at our son's future events. Thankfully, my ex was amenable to this and respected my wishes.

When he introduced a new woman into this dynamic, who also had suffered as a child of divorce, she turned out to be a saint in terms of continuing the cooperation between households. We discussed each other's needs openly, including my control needs over who was allowed to take my son for haircuts and other silly things that seemed so important at the time.

We had periodic issues but we strove to work through them cooperatively. Occasionally we had Thanksgiving and Christmas dinners together. We socialized at practices and games. I now view my son's stepmother as one of the greatest blessings in my life with her wonderful and generous natural gifts, and we continue to be dear friends to this day.

She made what was one of the scariest times of my life feel safe, because her foremost concern was what was best for her husband's son, which included considering what was best for me. The ongoing cooperation between the three of us required giving from us all, sometimes a lot of giving. I will be forever thankful to my ex and his wife for how much they gave.

Some fatherly advice from a family friend was of great benefit to my son's dad. This older man sat my ex down and told him to stay close and be a part of his son's life. The family friend passed on the lessons he had learned the hard way through his own divorce. Fortunately, my son's father listened.

We lived within walking distance until my son was thirteen. This made drop-off and pick-up easy and minimized confusion over which house the school backpack or basketball shoes were at. We also adopted the logic that gifts we gave our son were his and there were no constraints over which of his belongings he took to which house.

Even with cooperation, divorce is painful. There is no doubt about that, but your children still deserve to have their parents behave like adults. No matter who is at fault, strive to take the high road. No matter how hard your ex-spouse tries to drag you down to their level, try to be the adult and show your children that they are your priority. Let your kids remain children even though your marriage fell apart.

If you are a divorced parent, for the sake of not only your daughters but also your sons, keep an open relationship with your ex-spouse. If you allow your own pain to take priority over your children, you will be making them pay the price for your divorce. Remember, they are children. You are the adult.

One last point on the topic of minimizing conflict. Never speak ill of your ex-spouse to your children. When they are adults, they'll figure out who is who and what is what on their own. Don't break their hearts by telling them things about the other parent that they are simply too young to hear. They'll figure it out eventually. Remember, the truth prevails even though in this case you might wish it actually didn't.

Don't be surprised if your heart breaks the day your child realizes the fallibility of the other parent. I now understand why my mother gave me those presents from my dad all those years ago. She loved me and it was breaking her heart to see me in pain.

The second primary risk factor to children post-divorce is suboptimal parenting. You could easily think that if you were a decent parent before your divorce then that would continue as such afterward. However, the stress of the divorce alone can easily deplete a person's energy. Add to that issues with new housing and finances and the energy left to give your children can easily be depleted.

To combat the risk of inadvertent suboptimal parenting, it's essential to focus on encouraging open communication with your children. Assure them that you can handle hearing things from them that might be troubling them, even if it involves your ex-spouse and even if they think it might upset you. Give them complete answers to the best of your ability. Let them know you will always be there for them, whether that be to talk or hug or cry. Be their support and stability at a time that everything that they have come to depend on is changing.

The next risk factor for children post-divorce is a potential decline in economic stability. Even with cooperative parents, resources that were formerly shared to support one household are now split between two.

An article in the *Dartmouth Undergraduate Journal of Science* reports: "Custodial mothers often experience a significant reduction in their economic resources after divorce, 'retaining only about 50-75 percent of their pre-divorce income [as] compared to the 90 percent retained by noncustodial fathers.' The effects of income usually affect the families indirectly. For example, they often lead single families to move to less expensive neighborhoods with weaker schools, higher crime rates and less desirable peer groups. Financial support from noncustodial fathers can protect children from these potentially harmful influences and lead to more positive relationships with their children."[4]

Regardless of who wanted the divorce and how much each side fought to get custody, it is imperative that parents balance out finances to prevent the statistically supported indication that girls without daddies are being raised in economic circumstances that lead to greater risk factors at an already vulnerable time.

I'm still not certain how my mother managed financially post-divorce. I know she got $50 per month per child. Other than that, all I know is that money was never my concern. In fact, despite having lost all her savings as a result of my stepfather, she maintained one promise to me when it came to my ability to go to college. She always promised I would never have the excuse of money to quit efforts at getting a college degree. To this day, I still think that was the most perfectly worded promise. If I didn't finish college, it could only be because I quit. Of course, I graduated from college and it was not without having to call her for financial help.

The great example my mother set is that she shouldered the burden of any financial worries. Whatever they were, I never knew of them. I knew only the stability of a home and food and clothes and an occasional new toy. I can't imagine how differently my childhood would have been and how hopeless and helpless I would have felt if the burdens of the stability of a home were mine to bear as a child.

As for my financial circumstances after the divorce, I went to work full time, having worked just three days a week before the divorce. I had some guilt over not being at home as much for my son. As an optimist, I tried to focus on the benefits. I decided it would benefit him to see me dealing with work, dealing with contractors around the house, dealing with neighbors and schools, and so on.

Be careful here though. Do not turn your children into surrogates for a spouse. Share from a learning perspective but don't lean on your children as if they are your adult friends. You are their mother first and foremost. I also solicited extended family and friends to attend events that I might not be able to attend. Children learn that life is full of choices and alternatives. They might be disappointed at times, but important lessons can be learned even then.

Another risk factor post-divorce is remarriage, which for our purposes includes living together. Remarriage brings substantial new sources of stress to children. There are new relationships with the new spouse and potential step-siblings, renewed conflict with the ex-spouse as jealousies may arise, new housing arrangements, and new schools, to name just a few.

The biggest risk is that the child might feel like their relationship with their mother is threatened[5], which can easily occur with the mother's attention now divided among more people. Because a girl's relationship with her mother can be more important than a boy's at this time, girls tend to resist remarriage more than boys.[6] The statistics indicate that a great number of girls will be in this situation, as one of out of three children of divorce will end up living with a step-parent before the age of 19.[7]

Before you take the gargantuan step into remarriage, think carefully. Are you in an emotionally well-balanced place to be making a commitment that holds dramatic sources of new stress for both you and your children? Certainly you could be, and each individual will be different.

My suggestion is that you seek both personal and joint counseling first to make sure your relationship is healthy enough to withstand the pressures of a new marriage, the complexities of having stepchildren, and the addition of another ex-spouse into the mix along with your own ex-spouse. Invest this time and money for the sake of both you and your children. If the relationship is strong, it will get stronger through the due diligence you show before making a commitment. If this pursuit causes undue stress for either you or your potential new partner, listen for those alarm bells ringing.

And try not to be tempted into solving financial stress by marrying. The added stresses caused by this dramatic change can easily outweigh the financial stress you were attempting to alleviate.

Post-divorce my decision was to stay single. My experience with my mother's remarriage left me fearful of putting my son through a childhood with a monster in the house. I dated early on after my divorce but even the slightest problem that might suggest the man could turn into a monster sent me running for the hills.

Did I rob my son of an opportunity to have an additional father figure in his life or other experiences that may have benefitted him? I don't think so. I believe I saved him from a miserable childhood.

I was not in a position at that time to select a good candidate for a spouse or to have a healthy relationship. For me, the best choice was to stay single. You can look at it as if the glass is half full or half empty. As an optimist, I chose to look at the benefits of being a single parent and enjoy them. For the sake of your children, be careful. "Roughly 67% to 80% of second marriages end in divorce."[8]

Post-divorce, it is critical to remember that you are the parent. You can mourn the loss of your marriage but still limit post-divorce conflict. Strive to be as supportive as possible to your children and provide them the stability they need. Limit the appearance of financial concerns. To the extent possible keep other factors in tact such as school, family and friends.

Seek counseling prior to considering remarriage, if not sooner. If you can do these things, you have gone a long way toward providing your children an opportunity to mature into well-balanced adults, who ultimately can have healthy long-term romantic relationships.

One of my favorite quotes comes from a character in the television series *Criminal Minds*, "Scars remind us of where we've been, they don't have to dictate where we're going."

21.

Setting Goals

H ave you ever thought of setting written goals for yourself? Are you afraid to set goals for fear of failure? Perhaps you're concerned that others will think your goals are lofty and unachievable and you can't tolerate that judgement. Many years ago, I remember telling a boyfriend that I wanted to become a writer. His concerned response was to question whether I realized how difficult it would be to achieve that.

Setting goals requires courage. Remember? Never up, never in. Yet again, girls without daddies can feel at a disadvantage when it comes to setting goals. They are more likely to accept circumstances that others would not. They may be more prone to failure in relationships that sets them on a path that makes survival a priority above other loftier goals. Perhaps an early relationship, children and divorce all combined to divert them from the path of college. Look past your current circumstances, no matter how you got there, and see what you want for your life and believe you can achieve it.

Does setting goals really make a difference? According to a study conducted in 1979 on Harvard MBA students, the answer is yes. Those students were asked if they had goals. A total of 84 percent had none, 13 percent had goals that weren't written down, and 3 percent had written goals. Flash forward 10 years and how did those students fair? The 3 percent with written goals earned on average ten times those without goals. The 13 percent with unwritten goals earned on average twice those without goals. There are four primary reasons people don't set goals:

- They don't know it's important.

- They don't know how.

- They fear failure.

- They fear rejection and criticism from others.[1]

If the last two reasons don't scream "girls without daddies," then I don't know what does. My example on this point is my mother. She did not have a supportive father. She is a brilliant woman. However, she never went to college because she under-valued her brilliance. Also, she didn't value her aspirations as wor-thy of prioritizing over the needs of others – including mine.

Unbeknown to me, her father often criticized her for funding my college because I was, after all, only a girl. How could she ever overcome the perspective of her own father to see herself, only a girl, as worthy? I'm thankful she could withstand his criticism of her for my sake.

When I got my biggest promotion, her first comment was that she wished her father was still alive so she could tell him. I tried to give her some emotional support for her father's absence but she shook her head and confessed that she just wanted to be able to throw my success in his face. That was the first time I heard of his derogatory comments about her funding my college. If this story rings true to you, throw the nonsense that you are not worth it out the door. Then go outside and make a bonfire of it. You are definitely worth it!

Look at your life and think about what you want from it. When you do this, eliminate all the noise and negativity from the naysayers around you. Pretend you are your own daughter. What would you want for her? If you would want it for your daughter then why not want it for yourself. Take control and map out a path to achieve those goals so that when you are a little older you are not wondering, "What if?" When you feel little control over your life in your developmental years, it is easy to fall into a pattern as an adult of surviving versus designing your own future.

How do you dream big and set goals to achieve those dreams? First, let's look at key attributes of effective goals:

- Goals need to be specific. Specific goals actually reduce anxiety, disappointment and frustration because their specificity increases your likelihood of success.

- Goals need to find a good balance of difficulty and attainability.

- Goal timelines (or at least sub-goal timelines) need to be short enough that the goals feel relevant.

- Goals need to have value and meaning to you in order to keep you motivated.[2] It's one thing to want something but you have to want it badly enough to work for it.

With those attributes in mind, how do you go about writing effective goals? Dream. Measure. Benchmark. Celebrate.[3]

Dream about what you want for your future for 15 minutes then jot your ideal life down. Do you see yourself advancing your education and getting a better job? How much education? What kind of job? Perhaps your dream is entirely different from that.

Whatever your dream, write it down. Be realistic but don't limit your potential by setting your goals too low. Setting an achievable goal doesn't mean it can't be huge. If you're a girl without a daddy, it might be difficult to think outside your circumstances. You don't want to limit your dreams because your idea of what is achievable is limited. Although the key attributes of goals indicate they should be attainable, for girls without daddies I'd shoot past what you might think is attainable a little, and likewise allow yourself some room to revisit your goals as you learn more, possibly fixing any over-reaches.

Benchmarks, or sub-goals, should be established for each goal. Benchmarks break large goals into realistic components. Not only will this make your big dreams seem realistic and achievable, it will keep you motivated as you make progress through the benchmarks toward your big goals.

Measure means establishing goals and sub-goals in such a way that you'll know when you've achieved them.

Celebrate means write down how you'll reward yourself when you achieve each goal, and even each benchmark.

Through my young adulthood, goal setting was not my forte. I wouldn't call myself a butterfly in a tornado, but I certainly didn't have well thought out goals, let alone written goals. For example, I wanted to marry a rich man who would take care of me. Even if that were a best-laid plan, it would still certainly require some reevaluation as I matured from a little girl into a woman. At this point, that goal wouldn't even fall into a very long list of desires, let alone goals.

I wanted to go to college. Sounds good, but if I'd thought that goal through a little more I might not have spent three years in pre-med before changing to business. My purpose isn't to criticize my inadequate childhood goal setting skills, but rather it's to point out that some aspects of goal setting can require reevaluation, especially for beginners.

If you discover that the path toward your goal requires far more effort than you have motivation to match, that's not all bad. I'm glad today that I'm not a doctor because having headed far enough down that road I'm comfortable that I would not have been happy in that profession. Additional advance research may have achieved the same result but I don't view learning as a failure. Besides, life-long learning is a desirable goal.

Well into adulthood with my career progressing nicely, I shifted the focus of my goals toward self-actualization. I started evaluating what I wanted from life from the perspective of how I would look back at my life as an old woman. Will I look back at my life and smile? I want to be a happy, wise old woman that people love to talk to, as opposed to some bitter old nag who drives people away.

In short, my goal is to have a calm, peaceful heart. Now there's a goal whose achievability one could question. Did that stop me? No, it was important to me and I was willing to accept mistakes while progressing toward this goal. When I realize I've behaved in a way that doesn't lead toward my goal of a calm peaceful heart, I stop, reevaluate and reaffirm that is what I want. Then I look at my recent failure and learn from it.

If you fail to meet a goal, revisit the goal and the reasons why you failed. Has your motivation waned? If so, why? Is that goal still in your 15-minute dream, or do you need to reestablish your goals? Goals can change as you mature and grow. Failure can help you learn about what you really want in life. Failure is an opportunity to learn, not an excuse to give up on your dreams.

Set goals for your life. If you move from day to day, letting life drive you where it will, then you might end up someplace you don't want to be. I have had other goals in my life, some of which I achieved, some of which I reevaluated and changed, and some of which I'm still working on.

If you are a single mom who has to work, who has to take care of the kids and take care of the house by yourself, you must eke out enough time to dream, measure, benchmark and celebrate. Just pay close attention to setting realistic time frames for your goals, given the current limitations on your time. Take 15 minutes to dream and then set written goals and start your path toward fulfilling your dreams.

22.

Domestic Violence and Abuse

How would I react to the title of this chapter, given that I was once the subject of emotional abuse? Would I think it applicable to me? Would I hide from reading it because I wasn't ready to face what was happening to me? Would I read it eagerly hoping for an understanding of how I got where I am? Would I hope it would help me get out? I really don't know. I think it would depend on the day I was reading it. With those thoughts in mind, I'm writing the beginning of this chapter from a perspective that I think might have kept me reading.

How did I end up where I was? My relationship started out wonderfully. I was so happy. Then it made its way slowly through normal relationship developments. We had fights and would work things out. The fights became more frequent. His comments changed from focusing on the topic to focusing on my character. Comments about my character became more and more derogatory.

Problems quickly became solely due to my mistakes. Soon, things that previously hadn't been issues became issues. Nothing I could do would ever fix what was wrong. Before I knew it, the most horrible things would come out of his mouth and be about me, not solely about my actions but about me to the core of who I was as a person. Soon he was slamming his fists past my face into walls or doors. You get the idea. It didn't happen overnight.

Having some distance from this situation, I can easily stand outside the window and look in and wonder why the hell that woman (me) isn't doing something. But, I remember being inside the window being slowly beat down over time in a way that was almost indiscernible. Looking through the window or standing inside the house – that's the difference.

It's hard to find words to help that woman inside the house. Maybe she's not ready to hear them. Maybe she's so beat down that all she can hear are the words of her abuser. Perhaps she's been abused all her life and she doesn't even realize there is a different way to exist or be treated. Perhaps she's stuck in the cycle of abuse and just looks forward to the relief that comes when her abuser temporarily gets back to normal behavior. Maybe she thinks no matter where she goes, he will find her and that's she's safer soaking up the denigration. How do you reach this woman and let her know there are people that care, people that can help, people that can keep her safe?

Can she for a moment believe there is an existence in which she can smile and not feel afraid or worthless? If that woman is you, in a good moment, a moment where you feel a little strength, a moment where you might be out of the house so no one can overhear you, call this number: 1-800-799-7233. Don't hang up when they answer. Just stay on the phone as long as you can. If you can't make it through that first call, call again and then call again.

Emotional and physical abuse can happen to anyone – anyone. If it is happening to you, it isn't because you did something that caused it or that somehow you deserve it. It can happen to strong women, educated women, mean women, nice women – there are no exceptions. While girls without daddies might find themselves the subject of abuse more frequently, that doesn't mean they deserve it. It simply means they didn't get the training to help them avoid or escape from it.

There's an additional dilemma for women of faith. If you've been told that abuse is not a biblically supported reason for divorce, you are misinformed. Even if that misinformation comes from your church and you have been told you cannot leave your spouse solely due to verbal abuse or other forms of abuse, do not believe it. That is simply ridiculous.

There are no religious restrictions to divorce when abuse exists. "It is vital to note that there are genuine, necessary cases that warrant a separation or divorce. (Physical danger to one or more parties in the home, rampant chemical, physical, or verbal abuse, and cases of blatant, continued adultery, provide justifiable, understandable, and biblical support in the consideration of divorce.)"[1]

For the God I love, it isn't a question of whether divorce is permitted or forgivable. My God is in the stands screaming at you, "Get out!"

Now for the more typical part of a chapter on abuse. There are expert resources on the topic of verbal or physical abuse. At HelpGuide.org website there is a great article titled, "Are You or Someone You Care About in an Abusive Relationship?" which provides guidance on determining whether emotional or physical abuse exists and gives contact information for where you can get help. The US the National Domestic Violence Hotline is 1-800-799-SAFE.

Here are a few key excerpts:

"Are you in an abusive relationship? Your inner thoughts and feelings – do you:

- Feel afraid of your partner much of the time?

- Avoid certain topics out of fear of angering your partner?

- Feel that you can't do anything right for your partner?

- Believe that you deserve to be hurt or mistreated?

- Wonder if you're the one who is crazy?

- Feel emotionally numb or helpless?

"Your partner's belittling behavior – does your partner:

- Humiliate or yell at you?

- Criticize you and put you down?

- Treat you so badly that you're embarrassed for your friends or family to see?

- Ignore or put down your opinions or accomplishments?

- Blame you for their own abusive behavior?

- See you as property or a sex object, rather than as a person?

"Violent behavior or threats – does your partner:

- Have a bad and unpredictable temper?

- Hurt you, or threaten to hurt or kill you?

- Threaten to take your children away or harm them?

- Threaten to commit suicide if you leave?

- Force you to have sex?

- Destroy your belongings?

"Your partner's controlling behavior – does your partner:

- Act excessively jealous and possessive?

- Control where you go or what you do?

- Keep you from seeing your friends or family?

- Limit your access to money, the phone, or the car?

- Constantly check up on you?

"Emotional abuse: It's a bigger problem than you think.

"Not all abusive relationships involve physical violence. Just because you're not battered and bruised doesn't mean you're not being abused. Many men and women suffer from emotional abuse, which is no less destructive. Unfortunately, emotional abuse is often minimized or overlooked – even by the person being abused.

"Economic or financial abuse: A subtle form of emotional abuse.

"Remember, an abuser's goal is to control you, and he or she will frequently use money to do so.

"Domestic abuse falls into a common pattern, or cycle of violence:

- Abuse – Your abusive partner lashes out with aggressive, belittling, or violent behavior. The abuse is a power play designed to show you 'who is boss.'

- Guilt – After abusing you, your partner feels guilt, but not over what he or she has done. Your partner is more worried about the possibility of being caught and facing consequences for his or her abusive behavior.

- Excuses – Your abuser rationalizes what he or she has done. The person may come up with a string of excuses or blame you for the abusive behavior – anything to avoid taking responsibility.

- 'Normal' behavior – The abuser does everything to regain control and keep the victim in the relationship. He/she may act as if nothing has happened, or may turn on the charm. This peaceful honeymoon phase may give the victim hope that the abuser has really changed this time.

- Fantasy and planning – Your abuser begins to fantasize about abusing you again. He spends a lot of time thinking about what you've done wrong and how he'll make you pay. Then he makes a plan for turning the fantasy of abuse into reality.

- Set-up – Your abuser sets you up and puts his plan in motion, creating a situation where he can justify abusing you.

"Your abuser's apologies and loving gestures in between the episodes of abuse can make it difficult to leave. He may make you believe that you are the only person who can help him, that things will be different this time, and that he truly loves you. However, the dangers of staying are very real."[2]

Not necessarily related specifically to abuse, but in general for all women, consider self-defense training. In the chapter titled You Don't Need to Be Rescued by a Man, we discussed benevolent sexism. One of the categories of benevolent sexism is gender differentiation, which considers the effects of men's physical dominance over women.

Consider combatting this dominance by building your sense of physical security independently of men. Do this through self-defense classes. You can even watch videos on self-defense on the internet and learn tricks such as how to break free if someone is choking you, etc.

Consider having mace, bear spray or wasp spray in your purse, your car and in your house at strategic places. When you do these things, you will walk taller and might even actually ward off random attempts by others at physical violence simply by how you are presenting yourself.

In all cases, if you believe you are being abused please seek help! National Domestic Violence Hotline is 1-800-799-7233 (SAFE).

Epilogue

When all is said and done, this isn't a book about how to blame your absent father for all your woes. After all, life was never meant to be fair and anyone that told you otherwise undoubtedly set you up for major disappointments.

Sure, it would be nice if everyone was born to two supportive parents, everyone had clean water, plenty of food, free healthcare and whatever else they believe they are entitled. Shy of landing in those seemingly ideal circumstances, it does us no good to bemoan what we weren't given and it does us no good to blame a father we've potentially never even met. The purpose of identifying potentially negative behavior patterns that might stem from having an absent father is to learn how to grow past those negative crutches to healthy behavior patterns.

At one point in my career I was bemoaning to a co-worker how tough things were. This particular co-worker was an employee of mine but due to health reasons he previously had to step down from the job I now held.

I'll never forget how he looked at me and then simply said, "Who told you it was going to be easy?"

I sighed. I knew he was right. Often, those things we desire require the biggest fight to obtain and maintain. Why should I expect to have a high-paying prestigious job and at the same time think it would ever be easy? Similarly, why would anyone think it would be easy to evolve into a mature, independent well-balanced person after starting out as someone who came into this world not even knowing how to eat solid foods?

Things that we value in life will require effort, sometimes a lot of effort. I refer you to the chapter on setting goals. Set lofty goals. When you fall short, just dust yourself off and make another run at it.

You only live this life one time and when you get to the end of it I doubt you'll want your tombstone to read: "She didn't get far because her father was absent."

Instead, when you get to the end let it be with a smile on your face because you fought like a beast to get to the top of the mountain you wanted to climb.

Bibliography

DeMar, Gary. *Last Days Madness: Obsession of the Modern Church*. American Vision, 1999.

Dobson, James C. *Love Must Be Tough: New Hope for Marriages in Crisis*. Tyndale Momentum, 2007.

Harley, William F. His Needs, *Her Needs: Building an Affair-Proof Marriage*. Revell, 2002.

Krammels, Richard P. *Fear, Control, and Letting Go*. West Brow Press, 2013.

Lewis, C.S. *Mere Christianity*. Harper. 2009.

Morin, Amy. *13 Things Mentally Strong People Don't Do*. HarperCollins, 2014.

Norwood, Robin. *Women Who Love Too Much: When You Keep Wishing and Hoping He'll Change*. Pocket Books, 2008.

Rubin, Lillian. *The Transcendental Child*. Harper, 1996.

Segerstrom, Susan C. *Breaking Murphy's Law*. The Guilford Press. 2006.

Weatherhead, Leslie D. *Christian Agnostic*. Abingdon Classics, 1990.

References

1. Who Are the Girls Without Daddies?

1. "Fatherless Homes Now Proven Beyond Doubt Harmful To Children" Fathers Unite. http://fathersunite.org/statistics_on_ fatherlessnes.html

2. "Marriage and Family as Deterrents from Delinquency, Violence and Crime," FamilyFacts.org. http://www.familyfacts.org/briefs/26/ marriage-and-family-as-deterrents-from-delinquency-violence-and-crime

3. "The Consequences of Fatherlessness," National Center for Fathering. http://www.fathers.com/statistics-and-research/ the-consequences-of-fatherlessness/

4. Ibid.

5. Hope, S. (2010, May 30). "Risk and Resilience in Children Coping with Divorce," Dartmouth Undergraduate Journal of Science. http://dujs.dartmouth.edu/2010/05/risk-and-resilience-in-children- coping-with-parental-divorce/#.WJLlrXeZPeQ

6. "Fatherless Homes Now Proven Beyond Doubt Harmful to Children" Fathers Unite.

7. Dawn. (2016, September 17). "Single Mother Statistics," Single Mother Guide. https://singlemotherguide.com/single-mother-statistics/

2. Breaking Up is Hard to Do

1. "Absentee Fathers and How They Affect Women's Relationships," Fatherless. https://sites.google.com/site/elizabethsylvester37/

2. "Attachment and Adult Relationships," Helpguide.org. https:// www.helpguide.org/articles/relationships/attachment-and-adult- relationships.htm

3. Ibid.

4. "Understanding Insecure Attachment – Part 1: Ambivalent/ Anxious Attachment," Psych Alive. http://www.psychalive. org/understanding-ambivalent-anxious-attachment/?utm_ content=buffer1acc2&utm_medium=social&utm_source=twitter. com&utm_campaign=buffer

5. Shah, N., (2015). "Effects of Attachment Disorder on Psychosocial Development." Inquiries Journal Vol. 7, No. 02, Pg 2-3. https://www.inquiriesjournal.com/articles/998/2/effects-of-attachment- disorder-on-psychosocial-development?utm_expid=22625156- 1.8puQUbwARr-YDYLuXdNYXg.0&utm_referrer=http%3A%2F%2Fr.

search.yahoo.com%2F_ylt%3DA0SO8zGDN5lYSf0A88lXNyoA%3B_ylu
%3DX3oDMTExb25mYTN0BGNvbG8DZ3ExBHBvcwM1BHZ0aWQDR
EZENl8xBHNlYwNzcg–%2FRV%3D2%2FRE%3D1486465028%2FRO
%3D10%2FRU%3Dhttp%253a%252f%252fwww.inquiriesjournal.com
%252farticles%252f998%252f2%252feffects-of-attachment-disorder-
on-psychosocial-development%2FRK%3D0%2FRS%3Dy8dRnSeAnVXh
tugO0DGA_Aa6CnQ-

3. Will You Always Feel Fatherless?

1. Roman, N., (2015, September 2). "Study Reveals Most People Don't Feel Like an Adult Until the Age of 29," Science.Mic.

https://mic.com/articles/124772/study-reveals-most-people-don-t-feel-like-an-adult-until-the-age-of-29#.Gwo7rXAA5

2. Vajda, P. (2013, November 26), "Emotional Intelligence or Emotional Maturity," Management Issues." http://www.managementissues.com/opinion/6811/emotional-intelligence-or-emotional-maturity/

3. Hover, J. "Emotional Maturity," Scribd. https://www.scribd.com/doc/87132814/Emotional-Maturity.
Fitzmaurice, K. "Six Levels of Emotional Maturity - Emotional Maturity is Your Choice for Happiness," kevinfitzmaurice.com. https://kevinfitzmaurice.com/free-stuff/responsibility-issues/the-6-levels-of-emotional-maturity/
Capri, U. Dr. (2014, February). "Emotional Maturity: Characteristics and Levels." INTERNATIONAL JOURNAL OF TECHNOLOGICAL EXPLORATION AND LEARNING. Vol. 3, No. 1, http://www.ijtel.org/v3n1/359-361CRP0301P22.pdf

4. Allen, S. PhD, Daly, K. PhD, "The Effects of Father Involvement: An Updated Research Summary of the Evidence," Father Involvement Research Alliance. http://www.fira.ca/cms/documents/29/Effects_of_Father_Involvement.pdf

5. Cruz, V. (2015, January 13), "Who Needs a Daddy Anyway?" LiveRevBlog. http://liverev.org/blog/who-needs-a-daddy-anyway/

4. Judgement Causes Pain

1. Mayo Clinic Staff. "Narcissistic Personality Disorder." Mayo Clinic. http://www.mayoclinic.org/diseases-conditions/narcissistic-personality-disorder/basics/symptoms/con-20025568

5. Are You a Victim?

1. Firestone, R. PhD. (2009, September 30) "Don't Play the Victim Game," *Psychology Today*.

https://www.psychologytoday.com/blog/
the-human-experience/200909/dont-play-the-victim-game

2. Thompson, J. MS LMFT (2010 January 19). "Learned
Helplessness: You're Not Trapped," GoodTherapy.org. http://www.
goodtherapy.org/blog/therapy-learned-helplessness/

3. Garrett-Akinsanya, B. (2017, January 13). Growing
Up Without a Father: The Impact on Girls and Women.
(Insight News). http://www.insightnews.com/2011/11/03/
growing-up-without-a-father-the-impact-on-girls-and-women/

4. Jackson, L.M. (2010). Where's My Daddy? Effects of
Fatherlessness on Women's Relational Communication. (Master's Theses,
San Jose State University, San Jose California). As Cited in Uebelacker,
Courtnage, and Whisman 2003. http://scholarworks.sjsu.edu/cgi/
viewcontent.cgi?article=4763&context=etd_theses

6. Own Your Feelings

1. Bernstein, J. (2013, September 20). "Five Easy Powerful
Ways to Validate Your Child's Feelings." Psychology Today. https://
www.psychologytoday.com/blog/liking-the-child-you-love/201309/
five-easy-powerful-ways-validate-your-childs-feelings

2. Growl, J. Psy.D. "We Are Responsible for Our Own Feelings."
Psychology Today. http://psychcentral.com/blog/archives/2008/08/30/
we-are-responsible-for-our-own-feelings/

7. Making Others Like You

1. Bloom, L. and Bloom, C. (2011, December 12). "The Cost
and Benefits of Emotional Honesty," Psychology Today. https://www.
psychologytoday.com/blog/stronger-the-broken-places/201112/
the-cost-and-benefits-emotional-honesty

1. Smith, S. (2016, November 3). "Why Emotional Openness Can
Be Difficult and What to Do about It," A Plus. http://aplus.com/a/
why-emotional-openness-can-be-difficult?no_monetization=true

8. Do You Avoid Conflict?

1. Beckwith, L. Ph.D. (2015, July 14). "Common Conflict
Management Styles." http://www.sagu.edu/thoughthub/
conflict-management-styles

2. "The Consequences of Fatherlessness," National Center
for Fathering. http://www.fathers.com/statistics-and-research/
the-consequences-of-fatherlessness/

3. Jackson, L. (2010). Where's My Daddy? Effects of Fatherlessness on Women's Relational Communication. (Master's Theses, San Jose State University, San Jose California). p 31

4 Birkhoff, J. "Gender, Conflict and Conflict Resolution." Mediate. http://www.mediate.com/articles/birkhoff.cfm

5. Ibid.

6. Callahan, S. (2008, September 3), "Seven Personal Skills for Effective Collaboration," Anecdote. http://www.anecdote.com/2008/09/seven-personal-skills-for-effective-collaboration/

7. Rykrsmith, E. (2013, June 28). "How to Develop Collaboration Skills," QuickBase The Fast Track.

9. Do You Feel Worthless?

1. Capri, U. Dr. (2014, February). "Emotional Maturity: Characteristics and Levels." INTERNATIONAL JOURNAL OF TECHNOLOGICAL EXPLORATION AND LEARNING. Vol. 3, No. 1, http://www.ijtel.org/v3n1/359-361CRP0301P22.pdf

2. Tartakovsky, M. M.S. (2014, September 2). "When You Feel Worthless." Psychology Today. http://psychcentral.com/blog/archives/2014/09/02/when-you-feel-worthless/

3. "Bystander Apathy Experiment," Explorable. https://explorable.com/bystander-apathy-experiment

4. Tartakovsky, M. M.S. (2014, September 2). "When You Feel Worthless." Psychology Today. http://psychcentral.com/blog/archives/2014/09/02/when-you-feel-worthless/

10. Do You Feel Like a Failure?

1. Jerabek, I. Ph.D. "Perfectionism and Low Self-Esteem." Conscious Living TV. http://consciouslivingtv.com/spirit-health/perfectionism-and-low-self-esteem.html

2. Cruz, V. "Who Needs a Father Anyway? The Handicap of Fatherlessness Part 1." Live Rev Blog. http://liverev.org/blog/who-needs-a-daddy-anyway/

11. Finally, Emotional Maturity

1. Hover, J. "Emotional Maturity," Scribd. https://www.scribd.com/doc/87132814/Emotional-Maturity Fitzmaurice, K. "Six Levels of Emotional Maturity - Emotional Maturity is Your Choice for Happiness," kevinfitzmaurice.com. https://kevinfitzmaurice.com/free-stuff/responsibility-issues/the-6-levels-of-emotional-maturity/

2. Murray, J. PhD, (2007, January 23). "Are You Growing Up or Just Getting Older?" http://www.sonic.net/~drmurray/maturity.htm

12. Your Type of Guy

1. "Fatherless Homes Now Proven Beyond Doubt Harmful To Children," Fathers Unite. http://fathersunite.org/statistics_on_fatherlessnes.html.

2. Kortsch, G. Ph.D. "Fatherless Women: What Happens to the Adult Woman was was Raised Without her Father?" Trans4mind. https://trans4mind.com/counterpoint/index-happiness-wellbeing/kortsch4.shtml

3. "The Consequences of Fatherlessness," National Center for Fathering. http://www.fathers.com/statistics-and-research/the-consequences-of-fatherlessness/

4. Teachman, Jay D. (2004, January). "The Childhood Living Arrangements of Children and the Characteristics of Their Marriages." Journal of Family Issues 25: 86-111

5. Miles, M. (2006). "Father Presence Matters: A Case for Family." (Doctor of Ministry Thesis). Liberty Theological Seminary. Heather Antecol, Kelly Bellard and Eric Helland, Does Single Parenthood Increase the Probability of Teenage Promiscuity, Drug Use, and Crime? Evidence from Divorce Law Changes (Mimeo, Center for Research on Child Well-being, Princeton University, 2002), 11-14.

13. Using Sex to Get Your Man

1. Mancini, L. (2010, May11). "Father Absence and Its Effects on Daughters." Pg 11. (Thesis). Western State Connecticut University. http://library.wcsu.edu/dspace/bitstream/0/527/1/Final+Thesis.pdf

2. Muehlenberg, B. (2014, August 27). "Daughters and Their Dads: The Vital Relationship." Culture Watch. https://billmuehlenberg.com/2014/08/27/daughters-and-their-dads-the-vital-relationship/

3. Ibid.

4. Mancini, L. Op. cit.

14. Can Men Be Just Friends?

1. McKay, B. and K. (2015, October 20). "Can Men and Women Just Be Friends?" The Art of Manliness. http://www.artofmanliness.com/2015/10/20/can-men-and-women-just-be-friends/

2. Nicholson, J. M.S.W. Ph. D. (2013, May 1). "Can Men and Women Be 'Just Friends'?". Psychology Today. https://

www.psychologytoday.com/blog/the-attraction-doctor/201304/
can-men-and-women-be-just-friends

15. You Don't Need to Be Rescued by a Man

1. Glick, P. and Fiske, S.T., (1996). "The Ambivalent Sexism
Inventory: Differentiating Hostile and Benevolent Sexism." Journal of
Personality and Social Psychology. Vol. 70, No. 3, 491-512. Copyright
1996 by the American Psychological Association, Inc. Retrieved from
http://citeseerx.ist.psu.edu/viewdoc/download?doi=10.1.1.470.9865&r
ep=rep1&type=pdf

2. Ibid.

16. Are You Attractive?

1. Gottberg, K. "Self Esteem & Self Image – What's The Difference
& Why Does It Matter?" SMARTLiving365.com. http://smartliving365.
com/self-esteem-self-image-whats-the-difference-why-does-it-matter/

2. Kay, K. (2014, March 3). "Confidence VS Self-Esteem."
The Confidence Code. http://theconfidencecode.com/2014/03/
confidence-vs-self-esteem/

3. Romero, J. (2014, November 25). "Father Figure Wanted: the
effect of absence of a father in a woman's love relationships." The
composition of Happiness. Openlab at City Tech. https://openlab.
citytech.cuny.edu/the-composition-of-happiness-f2014/2014/11/25/
father-figure-wanted-the-effect-of-absence-of-a-father-in-a-womans-
love-relationships/

4. Selvarajah, A., Ph.D., "Self Esteem - The Problem Behind All
Problems." (2000). http://www.selfgrowth.com/articles/Selvarajah13.
html

17. Are You an Optimist or a Pessimist?

1. Goudreau, J. (2012, April 13). "Superstitions And Magical
Thinking: How Irrational Beliefs Keep Us Sane," Forbes. http://www.
forbes.com/sites/jennagoudreau/2012/04/13/superstitions-and-magical-
thinking-how-irrational-beliefs-keep-us-sane/#12f18bc42ca0

2. The Secret. Wikipedia.org. https://en.wikipedia.org/wiki/
The_Secret_(book)

3. Parashar, F. "Optimism and Pessimism," Positive Psychology.
http://positivepsychology.org.uk/optimism-pessimism-theory/

4. Shruti, S. and Mishra, S. (2014, June). "Optimism – Pessimism
among Adolescents – A Gender Based Study," Paper ID: 020144481.
International Journal of Science and Research (IJSR) ISSN (Online):

2319-7064. Volume 3, Issue 6. http://www.ijsr.net/archive/v3i6/MDIwMTQ0ODE%3D.pdf

5. Lara, S. and Sharma S. (2014, October). "Comparative Study of Optimistic and Pessimistic Attitude of Adolescents in Relation to Their Locality and Parental Encouragement," International Journal of Behavioral Social and Movement Sciences. Volume 3, Issue 4. (ISSN: 2277-7547). http://www.ijobsms.in/6dv3i4p11A%20SUMAN%20LATA%20%20p11A.pdf

6. "Fatherless Stats." Fatherhood Factor. http://fatherhoodfactor.com/us-fatherless-statistics/

7. Parashar, F. "Optimism and Pessimism," Positive Psychology. http://positivepsychology.org.uk/optimism-pessimism-theory/

8. (2010, August 11). "The Psychology of Happiness," Stanford Graduate School of Business. Case M-330. Pg. 6. https://www.gsb.stanford.edu/gsb-cmis/gsb-cmis-download-auth/352136

9. Wether, M. (2009, September 1). "Smile! It Could Make You Happier," Scientific American Mind. https://www.scientificamerican.com/article/smile-it-could-make-you-happier/

10. "The Psychology of Happiness," Op. cit. Pg. 12.

18. When Daddy Returns

1. Yoffe, E., (2013, February 18), "The Debt. When terrible, abusive parents come crawling back, what do their grown children owe them?" Slate. http://www.slate.com/articles/life/family/2013/02/abusive_parents_what_do_grown_children_owe_the_mothers_and_fathers_who_made.html

19. Faith as a Tool

1. Pack, D. "The Existence of God - Logically Proven!" The Real Truth. https://realtruth.org/articles/140710-001.html

20. Divorce is Ugly

1. Whiten, S., Rhodes, G., Stanley, S. and Markman, H., (2008, October 22). "Effects of Parental Divorce on Marital Commitment and Confidence," US National Library of Medicine National Institutes of Health. https://www.ncbi.nlm.nih.gov/pmc/articles/PMC2704052/

2. (2011, September 5). "The Impact of Divorce Upon Children – A Thesis Study in Grief, Trauma, and Stress Children Face When Parents Divorce," Order In the Quart." https://orderinthequart.wordpress.com/2011/09/05/the-impact-of-divorce-upon-children-a-thesis-study-in-grief-trauma-and-stress-children-face-when-parents-divorce/

3. Arkowitz, H. and Lilienfeld, S. (2013, March 1). "Is Divorce Bad for Children?" Scientific American Mind. https://www.scientificamerican.com/article/is-divorce-bad-for-children/

4. Hope, S. (2010, May 30). "Risk and Resilience in Children Coping with Divorce," Dartmouth Undergraduate Journal of Science. http://dujs.dartmouth.edu/2010/05/risk-and-resilience-in-children-coping-with-parental-divorce/#.WJLlrXeZPeQ

5. (2011, September 5). "The Impact of Divorce Upon Children – A Thesis Study in Grief, Trauma, and Stress Children Face When Parents Divorce," Order In the Quart." https://orderinthequart.wordpress.com/2011/09/05/the-impact-of-divorce-upon-children-a-thesis-study-in-grief-trauma-and-stress-children-face-when-parents-divorce/

6. Hope, S. (2010, May 30). "Risk and Resilience in Children Coping with Divorce," Dartmouth Undergraduate Journal of Science. http://dujs.dartmouth.edu/2010/05/risk-and-resilience-in-children-coping-with-parental-divorce/#.WJLlrXeZPeQ

7. (2011, September 5). "The Impact of Divorce Upon Children – A Thesis Study in Grief, Trauma, and Stress Children Face When Parents Divorce," Order In the Quart." https://orderinthequart.wordpress.com/2011/09/05/the-impact-of-divorce-upon-children-a-thesis-study-in-grief-trauma-and-stress-children-face-when-parents-divorce/

8. Cepeda, M. (2016, April 12). "7 Divorce Myths Debunked," Woman's Day. http://www.womansday.com/relationships/dating-marriage/advice/a6772/divorce-facts/

21. Setting Goals

1. "Harvard Business School Goal Story, Study about Goals at Harvard MBA Program, 1979" From the book, What They Don't Teach You at Harvard Business School, by McCormack, M., retrieved from http://www.lifemastering.com/en/harvard_school.html

2. Turkay, S. (2014). "Setting Goals – Who, Why, How." Harvard University. http://hilt.harvard.edu/files/hilt/files/settinggoals.pdf

3. Feinstein, A., (2014, April 8). "Why You Should Be Writing Down Your Goals," Forbes. http://www.forbes.com/sites/ellevate/2014/04/08/why-you-should-be-writing-down-your-goals/#1ece17dc2f14

22. Domestic Violence and Abuse

1. (2011, September 5). "The Impact of Divorce Upon Children – A Thesis Study in Grief, Trauma, and Stress Children Face When Parents Divorce," Order In the Quart. https://orderinthequart. wordpress.com/2011/09/05/the-impact-of-divorce-upon-children-a-thesis-study-in-grief-trauma-and-stress-children-face-when-parents-divorce/

2. "Are You or Someone You Care About in an Abusive Relationship?," HELPGUIDE.org. https://www.helpguide.org/articles/abuse/domestic-violence-and-abuse.htm#more

Made in United States
Orlando, FL
18 February 2023

30116925R00091